Wall Street's Buried Treasure

Wall Street's Buried Treasure

THE LOW-PRICED VALUE INVESTING APPROACH TO FINDING GREAT STOCKS

Harvey I. Houtkin

WILEY

John Wiley & Sons, Inc.

Published by John Wiley & Sons, Inc., Hoboken, New Jersey.
Published simultaneously in Canada.

For general information on our other products and services or for technical
support, please contact our Customer Care Department within the United States at
(800) 762-2974, outside the United States at (317) 572-3993 or fax (317) 572-4002.

Wiley also publishes its books in a variety of electronic formats. Some content that
appears in print may not be available in electronic formats. For more information
about Wiley products, visit our Web site at www.wiley.com.

Library of Congress Cataloging-in-Publication Data

Houtkin, Harvey I.
  Wall Street's buried treasure : the low-priced value investing approach to finding
great stocks / Harvey I. Houtkin.
      p. cm.
  ISBN 978-0-470-26067-8 (cloth)
  1. Stocks. 2. Value investing. I. Title.
  HG4661.H674 2008
  332.63'22–dc22
                                    2008020134

Printed in the United States of America
10 9 8 7 6 5 4 3 2 1

Contents

Preface

This book is derived from my many experiences observed and learned in my 40-plus years on Wall Street. My extensive dealings in many aspects of Wall Street's operations and techniques have made me quite an expert on the realities of this world. Unfortunately, these realities are all too often not pleasant ones for you, the investor/trader; nevertheless, they are realities that can, and do, affect you in the place you least like it—your pocket. Although millions of Americans are, and have been, involved in the financial markets, most do not have pleasant things to say about their experiences with "Wall Street." Yet, the opportunity and potential for obtaining wealth in this arena is exceptional.

Despite the fact that I was named "One of the Five in History Who Made It Happen on Wall Street" by CNBC on the eve of this millennium, I have had a passion for being a market "treasure hunter" for over 40 years. Considering the reputation I developed over the years as a leader in the electronic trading and day-trading world, many might find it unusual that I have always had a passion for low-priced value stocks. Call it an addiction or whatever: I love the adventure and profitability it has created for me over the years.

During the past 40 years, I have been a member of the New York Stock Exchange, the National Association of Securities Dealers (NASD), and various other stock and commodity exchanges, while for the past 20 years, I have probably been one of the most vocal critics of Wall Street, as well as one of its most vigilant reformers. I instigated major reforms into cutting spreads, decimal pricing, increased transparency, and enhanced market access, and fought for more open disclosure. I currently own a large NASD market-making firm, despite the fact that I am often critical of many market-making activities. All of my activities have been aimed at leveling the playing field for all market participants.

Long before it became fashionable to criticize the unfairness and misdeeds of the Wall Street community, I was pushing and fighting for reforms and changes. My trials and tribulations with fighting the Wall Street establishment are well known and have been documented in many books and articles written by various prominent authors and columnists. Rather than go into my extensive history of accomplishments and reform, I suggest you just Google me online for a host of details.

Once you read about me, it's easy to see that, simply put, I don't trust the conventional wisdom spewed by Wall Street and probably never will. Historically, there has been virtually no aspect of our financial community that has been trouble or scandal free. The problems and abuses of our financial system are so widespread and deep rooted that they go far beyond just Wall Street itself. Regulators, media, academia, and even our judicial system have done little to level the playing field for the public participant. Unfortunately, I no longer believe much can be done to further reform of our financial markets; the powers that be are just too powerful and their self-interest too enormous and entrenched. Rather than giving in or trying to confront these entrenched realities, restructuring the way you interact within the market by changing your fundamental way of thinking would probably be a much more practical and effective solution for you as an individual investor.

The vast majority of the so-called "experts" on Wall Street would consider most of the ideas I am putting forth in the following pages radical. Most of these experts as a rule espouse the conventional wisdom of Wall Street, which is designed to keep their self-serving game intact: "they" stay well fed and prosperous, while you watch your savings disappear.

With this in mind, I will be explaining some of the ways I have dealt with this reality in hopes of making the system work well for me. Remember, the name of the game here is *making money*—and that means as much money as possible, without giving away or losing our hard-earned wealth, but there are very few altruistic activities prevalent in the Wall Street arena. Money is the name of the game; they want yours, and they will do what they have to in order to get at it.

I believe that when you play the Wall Street game it is typically on their playing field. Wall Street experts have many advantages, using many illusions and ploys to get you to do exactly what they want. In order to win you must understand the situation and be able to think "outside the box." Don't lose hope. It can be done! You can do it by playing in an arena that the big boys can't and/or won't. Follow this text. Read it and you will learn a course of action meant for the average investor, one where most of the benefits can be derived directly by you. By its very nature, low-priced value investing possesses an edge for the "small" guy, and I hope to help show you the way.

Please note that all the opinions, representations, examples, commentaries, and statements contained in this text are my own, developed during my many years of experience in the financial community dominated by Wall Street. I believe what I say to be true and accurate. Others may disagree with my reasoning and strategy for a variety of reasons but, by and large, for selfish reasons. Therefore, read this text completely, and try to take heed and understand what I am saying and decide for yourself what seems sensible and logically true. I will try to expose you to my inner way of thinking by explaining my thought processes regarding low-priced value investing, how I did my homework, developed my strategies, and realistically found ways of implementing them.

With that said, please don't take any particular statement or statements, advice, or policy contained herein as a universal, absolute fact or reality. Wall Street and investing in general contain far too many variables for any particular theory to be taken as universally correct. Do your research and always watch out for yourself by checking out and verifying everything you feel is relevant to your situation, or may be questionable in your mind.

Playing Wall Street is an art, not a science. This text contains my opinions, realities, experiences, and personal observations of over 40 years in this arena. I hope you will find them helpful, and that they will make a lasting impression, and guide you to success.

Good luck!

HARVEY I. HOUTKIN
Aventura, FL
December 2007

Introduction

I don't believe there is a person on this earth who has not at one time or another fantasized about somehow or in some way finding a lost or hidden treasure. It is a dream that is almost universal among children and adults of all ages, colors, and creeds. The potential thrill of discovering a formerly lost or hidden store of wealth and making it one's own creates an excitement that is universal in nature.

The treasure can be in any number of forms: a pirate's buried chest of gold and jewels, sunken ships loaded with untold booty, or master works of art hidden and pillaged during years of conflicts and wars, just to name a few. Mel Fisher, probably the most famous treasure hunter of our time, inspired dreams of enormous instant wealth in people worldwide when in 1985 he discovered Spanish galleons that sank during a hurricane on September 6, 1622, near Key West, Florida. His $450 million treasure, which was ultimately retained after numerous lawsuits, is a reality that dreams are made of. Upon a closer look, however, we find that his "instant wealth" wasn't instantaneous at all and, as a matter of fact, it took Mel over 16 years of frustration, financial stress, and tragedy to accomplish his dream. Even great finds of buried treasure can have sizable costs and trauma, yet the dreams go on.

Thousands of modern-day treasure hunters still continue their search for all kinds of valuables. The Florida coast alone has a plethora of people in daily pursuit of sunken and lost treasures. Thousands of other people regularly go "treasure hunting" at garage sales and flea markets in an effort to find the treasure of a lost work of art, a missing copy of the U.S. Constitution (hidden under a cheap framed picture), or some costume jewelry that turns out to be genuine. Thousands of others routinely use metal detectors and other devices to comb vast areas of beach or other locations in the expectation of finding unknown treasures. It appears that the yearning of people to make big "scores" with a combination of a little hard work and a good amount of luck is apparently a universal theme, given all the stories you hear and movies you see today.

Unfortunately, most treasure hunters never realize the major score that makes their efforts economically worthwhile. If the entertainment value of an endeavor is considered meaningful to a treasure hunter, then that person might feel the effort expended was worth their investment of time and expense. However, since the hobby and hope value of the effort varies from person to person, there is no way of assigning a numeric rate of return for the investment in this enterprise. It seems pretty obvious that many people do ascribe a great deal of value to the pleasure aspect of treasure hunting because the number of them is ever increasing.

Never mind pie-in-the-sky hopes, though. After 40 years of evaluation and experience, I have found a territory so rich in buried treasure opportunity, it makes all other treasure-hunting opportunities pale in comparison. This area of treasure is so close to you it seems impossible, so rich in potential it seems improbable, so readily accessible it seems astonishing, yet so real and probable it is nothing short of amazing. Why would I tell you about this unbelievable situation and not keep it all to myself? A good question with a very logical answer. The area of opportunity I am referring to is a very specific type of investing: low-priced value investing, which is investing in stocks that few people even consider investment candidates and few "market pros" would tell you about even in the unlikely event they knew about them. The buried treasures you will be digging and searching for are called low-priced value stocks (LPVSs).

Perhaps one of the greatest opportunities to prosper that I have observed in my many years on Wall Street is in the intelligent commitment of capital in the LPVS arena. The returns I have earned on investments in these types of stocks have on many occasions made me thousands of percentage points in profit and significantly changed my economic life. Instead of breaking my back physically digging for various other kinds of buried treasure, I chose to work at finding low-priced "forgotten" companies and buying a reasonably large amount of these shares. Overall, I am proud to say this strategy has worked out exceptionally well for me over the years, and I believe the following text should demonstrate to even the most hardened skeptics to take heed of this market philosophy. The amounts of money to be made in this type of strategy surely could dwarf the returns on any other type of treasure hunting and outperform the returns on most types of conventional investing. For those of you seeking the adventure and willing to commit a little effort, the rewards to be had from disciplined low-priced value investing should more than take your mind off any other type of digging for buried treasure. It will also most surely get you thinking and reappraising your other mainstream Wall Street–type investments.

The following chapters attempt to familiarize you with the reality of Wall Street investing in general. This includes the actual difficulties one faces in venturing in the very competitive, slanted playing field of the financial markets. I explain the many different motivations and agendas prevalent in today's investment world. You will soon understand why following a low-priced value strategy makes sense versus more conventional investment strategies. The benefits of successful LPVS investing will become quite apparent. Then you will learn the nuances of maneuvering in this very special arena. You will gain from my examples, a way of thinking and approaching this very special market. The actual techniques required to increase your effectiveness will be discussed, as will the pitfalls and temptations you should try to avoid. Read this text carefully, because while many points I make may seem simple or obvious, they can be very significant toward your potential successes. By the time you finally absorb the information being put forth, nothing in this area should come as a surprise to you. I have attempted to dive deeply into the realities in this field by demonstrating and disclosing many of my experiences from the past 40 years.

Proceed with confidence.

CHAPTER

1

Overcoming the Conventional Wisdom

For the past four years I have spent the bulk of my time residing in the Miami/Ft. Lauderdale area. Unlike in the New York City area, where I was born, raised, and resided for most of my life, I began spending more time with people who are retired or semi-retired, having varying amounts of accumulated wealth, and who are quite anxious to talk about their financial and investment needs and wants. As an active trader and owner of a busy broker-dealer, I seldom had time to get involved with "average" retail clients, since that was never the primary focus of my business. Electronic trading and leveling the playing field on Wall Street occupied the majority of my time and thought.

Why Is It So Hard to Get Good Advice on Wall Street?

When looking back, what amazed me was how little the average guy seemed to know about the realities and inner workings of Wall Street or the financial community in general. Even acquaintances of mine who believed they were savvy and relatively informed about Wall Street realities soon found out otherwise after a brief "no-holds-barred" conversation. Simply put, most people now realize that making money on Wall Street using conventional wisdom, techniques, and strategies historically employed does not work. The combination of market reforms, electronic access, high-speed information flow, and the general distrust of the old ways of doing business have dramatically changed the realities under which we now trade and invest.

After over 40 years of being in the belly of the beast, I'm pretty sure few people know and/or understand more than I do about the realities of the market, especially concerning the inner workings of the equities markets. In general, people know they can't entirely trust their brokers but don't exactly know why. After all, they pay them plenty of commission dollars, so why do they so often decimate their portfolios? Why did the stock you just bought drop so precipitously right after you received your execution? Why did you pay more or receive less for the shares you just traded than did your best friend, who traded it at the same time? Why did that "hot tip" fizzle right after you bought it? How can you get greater returns than you are currently receiving? How come traditional "buy-and-hold" techniques so often spell disaster?

Many questions, few good answers. People often look to me for advice. Unfortunately, I do not like giving advice because it is a thankless endeavor. If you dispense advice and you're right…good, they seem happy, but why didn't you tell them to buy even more? If the advice turns out to be neutral…why did you tie up their money in a stock that was dead? They could have made more in a money market account. If they wind up losing a little money, you're a bum. And if they lose a lot, you're a crook, and they may file regulatory complaints against you or even sue. Almost everyone today has a son, brother, friend, cousin, or associate who is a lawyer always looking for a few more billable hours.

Therefore, dispensing market advice or assisting people in their stock market efforts be can problematic, to say the least. Since I usually don't handle retail accounts (with the exception of a few close friends), there typically isn't even a commission motivation. The reality is that for the average person, it is very difficult to get truly good advice about stocks. If someone really has great insight into the market and is a big winner, why would he tell anyone? He would buy it all for himself (you can never have too much money) or distribute that information only to people who could return the favor in other situations. The "gems" are usually long gone before you'll hear about them. By the time you find out, it's usually too late.

I have been giving these scenarios a great deal of thought and have come up with some theories and ideas about successful investing. Most people know me as the "father of electronic trading," but my love of low-priced value investing goes back much farther than my electronic day-trading history. There are major differences between "investing" and "trading." Simply put, trading involves profiting from intraday price fluctuations of actively traded volatile stocks, while investing usually means committing funds to a stock that you believe can appreciate significantly over a period of time. The problem with investing is "knowing" what to invest in and for how long. Everyone wants to invest in something that will go up quickly and make them lots of money with virtually *no* risk—and I'd like to lose 50 pounds eating a high-fat, high-sugar, high-carbohydrate diet, *but it isn't gonna happen!*

Take Note

Simply put, trading involves profiting off intraday price fluctuations of actively traded volatile stocks, while investing usually means committing funds to a stock that you believe can appreciate significantly over a period of time.

Most stock analysis is performed by trying to evaluate the potential risks in a situation versus the potential rewards. Some of the most brilliant minds in this and other countries spend thousands of hours and millions of dollars developing sophisticated models that try to successfully analyze stocks. Some succeed while others fail, and always to a greater or lesser degree. When an analyst at a Wall Street firm comes up with an idea, it usually gets disseminated to clients in the order of a their importance to the firm. The fact is that the larger, better-capitalized clients receive this "good" information long before less-capitalized clients do. But there are problems prior to the dissemination. First, the information: is it really any good? Second, by the time you receive it, how much has the stock already been impacted?

The preceding scenario leads me to the conclusion that most stocks that are generally well covered and followed by Wall Street trade in a "neutral zone." Stocks that have brokerage, institutional, bank, mutual fund, hedge fund, large retail, or media interest are usually trading in a well-established neutral zone. What I mean by neutral zone is a price level efficiently determined by the market and basically fairly valued because so many people know virtually everything about this stock. Enough participants are actively trading or invested in the shares, which assures that the current price in the market is essentially correct based on the numerous well-disseminated factors widely available. Naturally, the shares can and will fluctuate, but it will be in a neutral-zone range created by normal fundamental and technical factors. Events that can distort activity in the zone are such things as short squeezes (although many would argue that this is a technical factor), regulatory announcements, or inside information being improperly disseminated (remember Martha).

Take Note

Stocks that have brokerage, institutional, bank, mutual fund, hedge fund, large retail, or media interest are usually trading in a well-established neutral zone.

You must ask yourself: is the potential reward sufficient enough on a stock to justify the risk of owning it? Reward is determined by price appreciation (for the time being, I'll ignore the short side). The dilemma is that if most major stocks trade in a neutral zone, the potential price movements and therefore investment opportunities are very often "neutered." If many people know what is going on at a company, its value is more or less established; only surprises to the upside or downside should move the stock significantly, and you're not supposed to know those things. It's called inside information, and trading on it is very illegal. Therefore, you must ask yourself: is potential routine price appreciation enough to justify the risk of stock ownership? Traders can potentially profit from intraday swings on the price of a stock, but an investor should be looking for above-average price appreciation to justify holding a risk position. Remember, stocks go down, too, and you may very well earn negative returns.

A World of Neutral Stocks

Are you hoping some young analyst at a high-profile firm will recommend your stock in order to kick it up in price? Is the analyst powerful enough to create an industry-wide reevaluation of its multiple, or will appreciation come only through good old fundamental earnings increases? In actuality, only an active trader might profit from a quick move generated by a recommendation from a well-respected analyst. If you're an investor, you need good, steady results to move your stock higher over a period of time. Ask yourself how long such "great" companies as General Electric (GE), Pfizer (PFE), Intel (INTC), Coca-Cola (KO), Ford (F), and so many others have traded in narrow ranges and all too often to the downside. Was the risk worth the rate of return? It is likely that you will see these stocks double or triple, or is it more likely that over another five years you'll see merely pathetic results? These companies and thousands like them have been neutered!

Most stocks trading today on major exchanges (the New York Stock Exchange [NYSE], the Nasdaq National, and the American Exchange [AMEX]), in my opinion, have been neutered. They have reached a point of neutrality and have lost their investment appeal. Big upside movements in these shares will occur only by surprise (unexpected business events, etc.) or because they are being manipulated (legally, of course) by the powers that be for their various needs (elections, foreign bank discontent, market meltdowns, etc.). Today's competitive international markets are going to make it tougher and tougher for our companies to compete; all things considered, making money now is harder than ever. The long-term outlook for American industry is not always rosy and certainly not for every company. The conventional wisdom of buying and holding has proven itself to be a fairy tale created by characters far more sinister than any Mother Goose ogre. Hey, maybe the advocates of buy-and-hold should be neutered. But I digress....

Even with this negative scenario, life goes on. The sun will come up tomorrow, and we will still be here wondering how to play this

Wall Street game in a smarter, more effective way. Low-interest money market funds and stingy certificates of deposit can't cut it forever. Playing the market may be the only hope for truly getting and staying ahead, yet it can alternatively cause you to lose your head. Radical, unconventional techniques and strategies must be considered and explored as new ways of approaching today's marketplace.

Take Note

Radical, unconventional techniques and strategies must be considered and explored as new ways of approaching today's marketplace.

Concluding Thoughts

It has not been easy, but despite all the negatives of the post-2000 market meltdown, I have found an investing style and technique that has delivered results way beyond even my wildest expectations. By any standard of conventional or historical thinking, the theories of making money by investing the way I will describe here should alter your previous market notions and thoughts. In the next few chapters I will put forth for your consideration a new way of approaching the market, and perhaps you will find the treasure map of your dreams. I call my investment strategy "Uncovering Wall Street's Buried Treasures."

CHAPTER

2

Wall Street's Buried Treasures

Ever since my first job on Wall Street way back in 1967, I have always been infatuated and drawn to the unusually high profit potential of low-priced stocks. My first experiences on Wall Street included many memories of people making what seemed to be huge profits on small speculative low-priced issues often referred to as "penny stocks." It seemed so simple and exciting that I couldn't wait to throw my hat into the ring.

Low-Priced Value Investing

The thrill of being able to take a relatively small amount of money and turn it into what then appeared to be a small fortune was mesmerizing. Most likely, the reason it seemed so compelling was that I came from a family of modest means and the apparent instant wealth potential seemed to be a dream come true. Even with my dad's help, I would have very little money to play with. Low-priced stocks meant lots of shares for a small amount of money. The logic was simple; it is much easier for a one-cent stock to go to two cents, a nickel stock to reach a dime, or a quarter stock to rise to 50 cents than to wait for a $30 stock to become a $60 stock. In each instance there is a 100 percent price increase, but surely the penny-stock move was much more probable—or so it appeared. With a little luck and if things hit just right, one's financial life could change quickly.

I saw this scenario being played out almost daily back in the late 1960s, and I was drawn in by the intoxicating results I witnessed. I saw what I believed to be small fortunes being made by numerous customers of the small broker-dealer with which I was affiliated. I was only 18 or 19 years old at the time and probably a bit rambunctious, so naturally I made some mistakes and lost a good portion of my initial money. As it turned out, my losses actually became the best tuition money I ever spent. I was so upset with myself for being so gullible, greedy, and naive that I smartened up quickly. My main motivation, my new prime directive, was *not* to lose money; I couldn't afford that luxury. My objective was to try to identify undiscovered value in low-priced issues, shares that had a high probability of significant appreciation with little downside risk. As they say in real estate, the three most important criteria are location, location, location; in low-priced stock investing, it's value, value, value. This "zero tolerance for loss" technique worked well and in a matter of a few short years, the $2,000 stake my dad and I put together was worth many, many times the original amount, and we both started to get ahead of the game.

> ### Take Note
> As they say in real estate, the three most important criteria are location, location, location; in low-priced stock investing, it's value, value, value.

Criteria for a Good Low-Priced Value Stock

There are a variety of factors that qualify a company as a potentially good low-priced value stock. The criteria in some instances are quite defined, while often special situations may convince an investor that other factors should be taken into consideration. In my opinion, the basic criteria for a good low-priced value stock (LPVS) to be considered for accumulation are:

- Low price due to lack of market interest, stocks trading under $5 a share, or preferably closer to the $1 level, or even less.
- Very little trading or volume in the shares.

- No meaningful financial community research coverage.
- Original underwriter defunct.
- Relatively small capitalization (number of shares outstanding).
- High cash holdings with little or no debt.
- Low price-earnings (P/E) ratio or good reason for lack of current earnings.
- Sound fundamental business condition.
- Apparent management apathy.
- Good industry or field of business with decent prospects.
- Little market-maker interest or only smaller, weaker firms trading the shares.
- In regulatory compliance (Securities and Exchange Commission [SEC], National Association of Securities Dealers [NASD], state, etc.).
- Little current news being disseminated.
- Management or insider purchases of the company shares.
- Meaningful company share buybacks or "going private" attempts.
- Share price collapse not directly related to company events (e.g., Internet meltdown, subprime fiasco).
- Market manipulation: drawing down price on little volume and for no apparent purpose (bear raid).
- New management or shell rebirth.

The more criteria a company possesses, the greater the chance it will succeed as a good, low-priced value stock winner. Of course, some of the preceding criteria would apply to most good investment analysis, but you will notice that many would not be typical pluses in a conventional analysis. For example, while most analysts might very well consider high cash holdings, a low P/E, sound fundamentals, and good industry prospects, most mainstream analysts would usually ignore the bulk of the remaining. It's these remaining criteria that spell the opportunity in LPVS investing.

Why Good Companies Become LPVSs

What I learned early on was that there were "low-priced" stocks and there were "penny stocks." The differences were quite succinct and defined. Some low-priced stocks trade at a low price for seemingly inexplicable reasons. They, in fact, might be very good companies whose stocks were just trading in pennies for reasons not necessarily having anything to do with the fundamentals of the company. Alternatively, other low-priced stocks are really worthless "penny stocks" having little or no redeeming value and trade in pennies because that's all they're worth (or less). As a group, Wall Street in many instances has come up with a seldom-used term for low-priced stocks with a market capitalization of under $50 million, calling them "nano-cap" stocks. This term is not commonly used by most Wall Street professionals, and most on the street just combine them in the micro-cap category. For purposes of this book, many of the LPVSs would be included, at one time or another, in the nano-cap category.

Take Note

Wall Street in many instances has come up with a seldom-used term for low-priced stocks with a market capitalization of under $50 million, calling them "nano-cap" stocks.

For those of you not familiar with the various categories of market capitalization, it is a measure of a company's total value. It is often referred to as "market cap," and it is the total dollar value of all the outstanding shares in a particular company. It is estimated by determining the cost of buying an entire business in its current state. It is calculated by multiplying the number of shares outstanding by the current market price of one share of its stock. While there is no standard recognized definition of the classes of market capitalizations, it is common Wall Street practice that the market capitalization categories are as follows:

- Mega-cap: Market cap of $200 billion and greater.
- Large-cap: Market cap of $10 billion to $200 billion.
- Mid-cap: Market cap of $2 billion to $10 billion.
- Small-cap: Market cap of $300 million to $2 billion.
- Micro-cap: Market cap of $50 million to $300 million.
- Nano-cap: Market cap of under $50 million.

Good-quality, low-priced stocks often have a relatively small capitalization (number of shares outstanding) and potentially a very promising future. Several low-priced issues I have been involved with have traded at prices near, or even under, their cash on hand and often significantly below their book values. I am repeatedly shocked at the inefficiency of the trading markets that allow such distortions to exist. Yet, they often do and are disregarded by the condescending logic of many so-called "experts." The low price frequently disguises a company's real underlying value and, in effect, is a major part of the problem. Many corporate officers of a low-priced stock feel helpless to do anything about the low valuation and become complacent and/or frustrated over the situation. Others use this reality to buy back shares for themselves or their company at attractive levels. Occasionally, this low price enables corporate management to issue sizable amounts of super-cheap options to themselves. Depending on the ethical makeup of management, this may or may not be a problem.

There are several perfectly plausible reasons why a quality, low-priced company's stock is trading at its low level (in pennies):

- The company's original underwriter may have gone out of business or is no longer interested or capable of supporting the shares.
- The death of a large insider is causing the estate to be forced into selling a large amount of its very thinly traded stock into an illiquid, nonreceptive marketplace.
- Lack of market maker participation.
- Little or no analyst coverage.
- Disinterested company management.
- Extremely poor market conditions.

And so on. I call stocks in this situation the "forgotten" stocks—unloved, ignored, chastised by a cruel and uncaring marketplace.

For whatever reason, when good companies trade in pennies, most major market professionals and players lose any and all interest in them. Rather than viewing them as an opportunity to increase their position, they often become an embarrassment to a portfolio manager. Many times, portfolio managers will look to rid themselves of these low-priced, poorly performing shares and get them out of their portfolios regardless of fundamental value. They are more concerned with the embarrassment of owning these losing positions in their portfolios than doing the right thing. After all, their jobs may be at stake. This scenario feeds on itself. As the stock declines further and further in price, it causes more and more forced liquidations because additional people then begin to "throw in the towel" and the stock price is forced yet lower. With the culmination of year-end tax selling, often this unrestrained selling breeds selling and results in a share price that can often be within earshot of zero.

To further exasperate this scenario, very often market makers "lean" on (aggressively sell short) the shares of troubled low-priced issues to help accentuate the stocks' rapid decline. They try to establish "short" positions, then put more and more downside pressure on the shares in the hope of "breaking the back" of the stock and then buying the shares back for almost nothing. The only upside to this scenario is that market makers are very often among the most unreliable people I ever had to deal with, and all too often get themselves in major jams when they find themselves heavily short into a sound situation, and a major "short squeeze" develops.

Most low-priced and penny-stock market makers seldom analyze the companies they trade and rarely establish investment positions, even in the best of the low-priced issues they trade. They are usually more than happy to supply the customer all the shares they can acquire for a small markup. To these market makers, low-priced/penny issues are just numbers. The type of market-making operation that trades these issues usually trade them as numbers and seldom know very much about the companies themselves. Many of these market-making firms trade literally thousands of these low-priced/penny issues, with little concern for the underlying fundamentals. Many fine companies have experienced the shame and pain of having their shares traded mercilessly lower in this low-priced/penny-stock environment for extended periods of time in their public trading history. These companies' managements are very often embarrassed by being referred to as penny stocks, and for good reason. These truly victimized companies—the ignored, overlooked, and forgotten—are in reality the *buried treasures* I am referring to. Uncovering (digging up) these opportunities can create a potential for wealth that few other market opportunities could ever approach.

True Penny Stocks

Alternatively, true penny stocks are often created from the very start to be a low-priced issue intended to be traded in pennies. Very often, the company and/or its promoters want to have the shares trade in pennies for a variety of reasons. Primarily, promoters find it easier to tout low-priced penny issues than to promote higher-priced securities. Penny stocks all too often become vehicles for abuse. Many unsavory characters often use the penny-stock arena to perpetrate massive fraud on countless numbers of unsuspecting public investors (you've watched *The Sopranos*, haven't you?). Penny stocks are touted in market letters and on Internet sites, and often have unscrupulous brokers spreading stories and rumors about these companies. My experience tells me that most, if not all, of these penny-stock promotions are scams, and the only people making money on them are the promoters, market makers, and a few lucky traders. The fact that so many people have been shafted by penny-stock promotions is a major reason why investors frequently shy away from all low-priced or penny-priced issues.

The ability to distinguish between the legitimate low-priced value issues and the bogus penny-stock scams can be the difference between wealth and disaster. The object of the next few chapters is to educate you to identify low-priced value, accumulate positions, and hopefully prosper, while learning how to avoid the often-tempting penny-stock scam. Examples will be given of several major winners that I have had in these types of stocks from 2000 to 2007. I also discuss my reasoning, trading techniques, and liquidation (exit) strategies. You probably know that most of this period was not a particularly good time for the market. Many people would say it stank, yet the returns on these stocks in several cases significantly exceeded 1,000 percent with little risk, to my way of thinking.

Understanding LPVSs

For purposes of this book, please be advised *one should always stay clear of true penny stocks*. My experience shows that virtually all of them are scams and they almost never work out as an investment. Occasionally, a nimble trader may be able to extract a large gain out of a penny-stock promotion, but seldom do investors ever make money holding these securities for more than a very short period of time, and they do so usually at great peril. In general, penny stocks are for suckers and fools and should be avoided at all costs. Instead, there are a variety of factors that qualify a company as a good low-priced value situation.

Most informed people would agree that what I just stated was the obvious; however, it is this general distrust of penny stocks that very often creates the unbelievable opportunities in some low-priced issues. The fact is that so many informed people shy away from low-priced securities because they blend them in with worthless penny stocks. Tremendous values and opportunities are often waiting out there for those who can look beyond their preexisting beliefs. If you are willing to expend a little effort and have some vision of the future, you should be able to sort through the list of low-priced issues and select a few of the companies that have been unmercifully beaten down (for any number of reasons) and pick a few candidates suitable for speculative investments.

Yes, some of your selections may turn out to be wrong and you may lose some or all of your invested dollars in that particular stock, but never more than 100 percent (low-priced stocks are not marginable). However, a good pick of a low-priced issue can return thousands of percentage points. Keeping a diversified portfolio of several high-probability, low-priced issues is the way to go about playing in this arena. Some of the most incredible gains I ever captured in the stock market came out of the often-scorned low-priced securities world. Despite the enormous potential results from well-thought-out investments in the low-priced arena, mainstream Wall Street continuously discourages the general public from venturing into these waters. They seem to have a problem when clients want to invest in good stocks at the very bottom of the market cycle but have no reservations about recommending relatively worthless, speculative stocks (e.g., biotech, Internet) trading at astronomical levels despite their lack of fundamental value.

Take Note

Keeping a diversified portfolio of several high-probability, low-priced issues is the way to go about playing in this arena.

Most brokerage firms have many restrictions on clients' purchasing low-priced stocks, making it prohibitively expensive and inconvenient to transact in these securities. The majority of brokerage firms absolutely prohibit any broker from recommending any penny stock trading under $2 a share and often even under $5 a share. Brokerage firms cannot and will not extend margin on the purchase of low-priced shares. They do not distinguish between a low-value-priced stock and a true penny stock. Brokers are told to warn their customers and often do not accept orders in low-priced issues or penny stocks. Most large firms universally consider any stock under $5 to be highly speculative and place severe restrictions on transacting business in these securities. (Ironically, some firms have reluctantly eased some of their restrictions on low-priced issues because so many of their underwritings and offerings have fallen so precipitously that they have, in fact, become penny stocks.)

Regulators also make life difficult for the low-priced stock. For example, when a Nasdaq-listed stock trades under a dollar for a period of time, they seek to delist the security from the Nasdaq National Market and relegate it to the bulletin board or, even worse, the dreaded pink sheets. What effectively happens after a delisting is that many mutual funds and other institutions are forced to liquidate these low-priced holdings, creating an even larger drawdown in the prices. While it is true that in some cases these companies may be on their last leg, many do persevere and come back with percentage gains that will knock your socks off. The reality is that Nasdaq very often, by its ill-advised actions, creates tremendous opportunities for the sharp value seeker selectively analyzing these potential candidates.

LPVSs versus Conventional Investing: Why Is Everyone Invested in Wal-Mart at $52 and not Lucent at $0.60?

The basic difference between investing in a good-value, low-priced issue and a more mainline recommendation from an established Wall Street firm is that the properly picked low-priced issue in general has a vastly greater upside potential (percentage-wise) than a well-followed standard security. Most securities traded on major exchanges or Nasdaq usually are followed or covered by at least a few brokerage houses, research departments, mutual funds, bank trust departments, insurance companies, and/or other informed analytical people. They disseminate their findings to their ultimate client, who then purchases or sells the particular security. The extensive interaction of informed buyers and sellers usually causes the price of a security to settle at relative equilibrium.

Take Note

The basic difference between investing in a good-value, low-priced issue and a more mainline recommendation from an established Wall Street firm is that the properly picked low-priced issue in general has a vastly greater upside potential (percentage-wise) than a well-followed standard security.

In today's world of instantaneous communication and computerized efficiency, analyses of a company's prospects are usually pretty accurate and quickly disseminated. This well-distributed information allows investors of all sizes to make informed buy/sell decisions almost instantly. Prices of the underlying securities adjust quickly as information flows through the system. Companies today are more concerned than ever to properly disclose required data to the investment world in a timely fashion due to the large penalties they face if they don't. What the above scenario adds up to is the reality that many stocks today trade in a narrower price range because of the efficiency and transparency of today's stock market.

Narrower, less volatile trading in many securities to a great extent reduces profit potential. If the pricing mechanism is efficient, discovering a truly undervalued stock is very difficult. Therefore, if upside potential and returns are reduced, why then invest in these stocks? The answer to this question is thought provoking.

Take Note

Many stocks today trade in a narrower price range because of the efficiency and transparency of today's stock market.

These realities leave the world of investing in low-priced securities primarily to aggressive individual investors who are willing to arrange their affairs in a way that enables them to take advantage of this opportunity. Just as it is a fact that major corporations don't usually invest in ocean salvage or treasure hunting, low-priced value investing is an opportunity left for the few bold adventure-seeking people who aspire to discovering the potentially huge rewards. Understand that while there are significant risks involved when putting your investment dollars into low-priced securities, if proper due diligence is exercised in the making of reasonable investment choices, the rewards can and often are exceptionally large. If I am going to take the risk of tying up my money in a stock, I want and expect to be rewarded handsomely if I am right. I'm a big boy and willing to accept losses when I make mistakes or exercise bad judgment. However, if I do my homework and am fortunate enough to choose a winner, I expect to be rewarded handsomely. I'm talking about many percentage points of gain: 50 percent, 100 percent, 500 percent, and 1,000 percent or more is not an unreasonable expectation when investing in low-priced securities. If I do not believe this is possible and probable, why invest? That's why I see so little logic in buying what I call the neutral stocks. If these often well-known securities offer only relatively limited price appreciation over time, why bother? The past few years (2000 through 2007) have been a perfect example of the fact that so many well-known, widely held, investment-grade stocks have languished in a neutral zone.

For example, Wal-Mart Stores (symbol: WMT), one of the largest, best-run companies in the country and the world has been, at least in my eyes, a major disappointment to investors who have committed billions of dollars to this stock. In the past six years, Wal-Mart's shares have traded in the range of $42 to $61 a share. If one bought into WMT at the midrange price of $52, the stock fluctuated a mere 10 percent maximum over the five-year period, and not necessarily in the direction an investor would want. Even if you add back the tiny, less than 1 percent annual dividend, the potential profit from this stock, even in a best-case scenario, was about 10 percent total over a five-year holding period. In my eyes, this kind of return is unacceptable. Despite the fact that WMT had double-digit growth in both earnings and sales, the price of the stock languished because the perceived multiple for the shares collapsed from 59 to 23. Why? The answer is that the increased growth and sales were well anticipated by the vast number of entities that closely follow the company. At least 30 analysts actively cover WMT, with somewhat differing opinions. At the time of this writing, only 3 analysts rated the stock a sale/underperformer, while 18 geniuses suggested that it was either a buy or a strong buy. Nine other bastions of knowledge were fence-sitters advising their followers to "hold"…whatever that means. Hold for what?

The point is that even a stock as important as WMT in today's market is probably not worth bothering with if one is looking for significant appreciation in his or her equity risk portfolio. To tie up money in an equity investment that has little upside potential is foolishness. Over the past six years, you would have been much better off buying a five-year note even at the stingy 4 percent return rate typically available—at least you could rest easy at night. Your compound return would have been much greater than many of the mainstream equity investments offered and promoted at most Wall Street establishments. Unfortunately, all too many of the followed stocks fall into a similar scenario as WMT. Worse yet is the fact that so many mainstream stocks of the past few years have declined so precipitously that they have not yet even come close to attaining their previous highs and, most likely, never will.

Take Note

Many mainstream stocks of the past few years have declined so pre-cipitously that they have not yet even come close to attaining their previous highs and, most likely, never will.

Lucent Technologies (symbol: LU; now Alcatel, symbol: ALU) was the most widely held blue-chip stock that came out of the AT&T breakup (formerly Western Electric) and was a perfect ex-ample of a low-priced opportunity. Between 2000 and 2004, LU fell from almost $90 a share to $0.60 a share and then rallied back to almost $5 a share. Will ALU ever see $90 a share again (adjusted for the merger) or exceed that price to give a long-term holder a profit? Not likely! Disaster like this is never corrected. However, if one looked at this stock from a different perspective, they could have seen the opportunity in the shares and gotten involved when it became a low-priced issue. When the Lucent shares traded under $1, down to $0.60, a tremendous opportunity emerged. Yes, there appeared to be high risk at the time, but any positive event or per-ceived positive development could (and did) vault the stock price enormously, especially from its then current price of under $1 a share. Literally hundreds of millions of shares turned over under $1; a person could have easily accumulated whatever size position (in dollars or shares) they desired to own. The rally back to almost $5 a share, while meaning little to the long-term conventional in-vestors who were still holding their high-priced positions, meant enormous returns to the low-priced stock investor who pocketed up to 800 percent returns in a few short months. Remember, a purchase of the shares at under $1 meant one could only lose no more than $1 a share, the amount of their investment. However, a rather minor rally in the shares relative to the historical price of the stock created an overwhelming price appreciation on a percent-age basis. Little downside with enormous upside potential...that's my idea of smart equity investing! Despite this obvious logic, the number of people buying in at or near the bottom ($0.60 to $1) was inconsequential relative to the masses who chased this stock at the 60s, 70s, 80s, and 90s price level.

Take Note

Little downside exposure with enormous upside potential—that's my idea of smart equity investing!

LPVSs and the Institutional Investor

The reality is that most of the investment money today in the market is handled by professional money managers who control literally trillions of dollars. The sheer amount of these dollars requires them to usually invest in larger-cap mainstream securities, companies with massive market capitalization and many millions, perhaps billions, of shares outstanding. These institutions and funds couldn't possibly seriously enter into the world of low-priced stocks because they would never be able to commit even a tiny portion of their assets without distorting the potential opportunity. Even if they did buy a relatively small amount of a particular issue and it went up dramatically, it would have an inconsequential effect on the overall portfolio performance. In reality, only a handful of small micro-cap funds regularly invest in low-priced securities. These funds usually have only relatively small amounts of capital compared with larger mutual funds and often close them out "early" to "new" investors. They often refuse to accept new capital because it is difficult to be efficient in a market that cannot readily provide enough liquidity for significant dollar amounts of new investment.

Low-priced value stocks are often not available in large enough quantities to satisfy the appetite of a large fund manager. For example, if a micro-cap fund raises $100 million to invest in micro-cap stocks, committing even 1 percent to 2 percent of their assets to a position would require the purchase of $1 to $2 million dollars worth of often very thinly traded stocks—no easy task. While the rewards could be exceptional, the opportunity cannot be widely disseminated or acted upon by competent micro-cap money managers. Therefore, the opportunity to find and invest in a competently managed fund of this sort is not often readily available, and most people are relegated to invest in the more common large- and mid-cap equity funds. There are a few well-run micro-cap funds in existence but most of the good ones that I know of have stopped accepting new funds. The reality is that most money managers couldn't play in this arena even if they wanted to. Too bad for them, but good for you as an individual if you are prepared to do your homework (to be discussed in the next chapter).

As a matter of fact, it is usually large institutional investors that are the source of most low-priced stock opportunities. Money managers usually care about one thing: self-preservation (their job). If bad news or anything perceived to be disappointing is announced about a security they hold in their portfolio, many money managers in general run for the hills and often indiscriminately enter market sell orders to void their portfolio of any stock that may prove embarrassing. Why answer questions or explain the position if it can disappear before the end of the fiscal quarter with only a minuscule effect on the overall portfolio performance? Their bonus might not even be affected. This "just sell it" attitude is the reason why these low-priced stocks don't just go down—they get gutted. These forced liquidations can often create fabulous low-priced opportunities for the astute investor because scared money managers wind up throwing out the baby with the bathwater. Perhaps not always on the first day of the debacle, but soon after the selling barrage begins, opportunity may come knocking.

Their Overreaction Can Spell Your Opportunity

Disappointing or bad news is many times in the eye of the beholder and not every money manager/analyst is the sharpest pencil in the bucket. If the problem the company is experiencing is not an obviously fatal one, accumulation of these severely depressed shares can be a tremendous opportunity. Usually, if the price of the victimized shares falls below $1, it may go lower yet because, as discussed previously, many potential buyers may, in fact, be precluded from buying and/or owning so-called penny stocks. Often, when people become irrational, that is the time when the greatest opportunities present themselves.

You must develop confidence in your own decision making and be prepared to act, even if it means going against the herd.

> ### Take Note
> You must develop confidence in your own decision making and be prepared to act, even if it means going against the herd.

Very often, the market overreacts to announcements of negative news. Almost daily, at least one or more companies are dramatically impacted by the market's reaction to a perceived negative development. These negative developments can come from a variety of sources. Perhaps the company business is unexpectedly down for the quarter or a lawsuit has been filed against it for any number of reasons. An officer's unexpected resignation or downgrade by an analyst can cause a major downdraft in the shares of a company. A recall of a product or a government investigation of some aspect of a company's operation can spell disaster for a company's shares. On balance, any number of events can cause a serious decline in a company's shares. A clear-headed evaluation of these apparently negative events can often expose a tremendous investment opportunity. If the downdraft brings the target company's shares into the low-priced stock arena, the opportunity for large-percentage gain is even more pronounced.

When a stock drops down from a relatively high level into the penny-stock zone, the overriding decision as to whether to invest is dependent on the company's ability to survive. The news is negative, the reporters are make things look even worse, institutions are selling aggressively, margin calls are being sent out, regulators are all over the company's management, rumors are flying, shorts are piling on, and, in general, the world looks like it's coming to an end. This is probably a good time to start nibbling on the shares. Unless you are absolutely sure there is no hope for the company (that it cannot survive fundamentally), buying shares into a meltdown makes sense, especially if you believe the company has the wherewithal to survive. Where there is life, there is hope. If the company can ride out the current problem and turn itself around, the shares can rise to several times this depressed penny level and make one a substantial return. Remember, in the Lucent example, the survival of the company financially was seldom in doubt even at the most tense moments, and the shares rose from well under a dollar to just under $5 in a short period of time after the collapse. The reward more than compensated for taking the risk.

Buying a stock that is in the process of rapid decline is a very risky proposition despite what may appear to be a bargain-basement price. For example, while Lucent was in the process of collapsing from $90 a share to under $1 a share, there were many times it looked like a screaming "buy." I remember when a friend of mine who was long the shares at the $60 level and who watched it trade up to $90 told me he dejectedly asked his broker (a well-respected major Wall Street firm) whether he should buy more when it declined to $34 a share. The broker's reply was that at the $34 level it was a slam dunk, an unequivocal "yes." Within weeks, the stock bottomed at under $1 a share. Was conventional wisdom right or wrong?

Some on Wall Street say that investing in stocks that are rapidly collapsing is like trying to "catch a falling knife," and in many cases this is very true. Often, you will get bloodied. My view—sometimes considered a little simplistic—is that a stock selling at under $1 can only go down less than $1, while its upside potential could be limitless. It is true that while you may only lose less than a dollar, that amount still represents 100 percent of your investment, and therefore, for risk evaluation purposes, one must consider the dollar amount of the entire investment when committing. Remember, stocks in decline tend to continue lower until a compelling reason or circumstance allows them to bottom and then hopefully trend higher. The LPVS tends to make the entry point easier because it simply can't go much lower, at least on a price basis.

Even at times when a company's stock plummets to the low-priced/penny-stock level and the company eventually does go out of business or even bankrupt, the shares still have a potential to reverse and rise once again. The fact that a company files for bankruptcy does not mean the shares are worthless, even if they trade down to a few pennies. Often, the reason they go down to pennies is the belief that there is nothing left for the stockholders and the shares will be totally worthless, and many times that is the case. However, on occasion, some companies go bankrupt or are forced into bankruptcy for reasons that very well might allow for a comeback (at least in its relative share price). For example, the Trump Hotels & Casino Resorts Inc., after falling into a cash crisis, filed for chapter 11 protection of the bankruptcy law in 2004. The shares immediately plummeted from over $3 a share to under $1. The New York Stock Exchange, showing a great deal of concern and compassion for the company, routinely and immediately delisted the shares, and they were delegated to the abyss of being traded on the pink sheets. After trading for a short period on the pink sheets, several market makers started to have it trade on the Nasdaq bulletin board, considered to be but one notch higher than the pink sheets in the minds of some. For weeks, the shares traded heavily in and around the $0.50 range, even trading as low as $0.17 in August 2004. Once again, investors could have acquired all the shares they reasonably could desire. The stock's average daily volume after the bankruptcy announcement was hundreds of thousands of shares, and at times several million shares traded on a single day. In December 2004, word came out about a possible restructuring that would give the stockholders some value in a post-bankruptcy reorganization. While nothing yet had been finalized, the shares of Trump (DJTCQ), in a matter of days, rose to well over $2 a share. While this price still did not even come close to the vicinity of the stock's all-time high (for the LPVS range it was trading in), the price represented a potential profit of over 1,000 percent, depending on one's specific entry purchase price.

Remember, even in bankruptcy, some companies' shares offer tremendous upside opportunity if certain corporate criteria are still being met. Occurrences like DJTCQ are not uncommon and are out there for those of us who do the research necessary to get in at the low-priced level.

Take Note

Even at times when a company's stock plummets to the low-priced/penny-stock level and the company eventually does go out of business or even bankrupt, the shares still have a potential to reverse and rise once again.

3

Doing Your Homework

Discovering a great low-priced value stock (LPVS) candidate is a never-ending search not unlike that of the real-world treasure hunter. Investors must constantly keep their eyes and ears open for ideas that can lead to potential candidates for investment. Good ideas can come from a variety of sources, including personal life experiences and simple discussions with friends and associates in the ordinary course of the day. Usually, there are no shortages of tips floating around the office cooler or on the golf course. The innumerable tout sheets and market letters available today are out of control, and they are usually pushing garbage penny stocks.

Staying Away from Bull

How many times have you heard about an investment opportunity and the word *they* comes up more often than you think reasonable. "They" say this or "they" say that, and no one ever really knows who "they" are. Many times, it is done deliberately to create mystery or to give the appearance that something is such big news that one could never tell you who it is coming from because of the aura of insider information. Who are "they"? No, seriously, who are they and what gives them the ability to know this great information that no one else seems to have heard? Furthermore, why are they telling me?

Why are they bestowing this big favor on little me? Why are they risking potentially serious legal problems by telling me something of substance that probably would be considered insider information or worse? Beware of the information. Santa Claus comes only once a year, and if he were disseminating insider information, you would probably only be able to visit him at the North Pole Penitentiary.

When searching around for an appropriate LPVS, you will probably come across hundreds, perhaps thousands, of low-priced stocks that qualify on a price basis for consideration as an investment candidate. Psychologically, many people love the concept of buying low-priced securities, especially those trading under $5, because of the large potential gain that would occur even if the stock just went up a small amount numerically. As discussed previously, the percentage of profit available through relatively small numeric moves could be enormous, and that makes them very tempting. The greed factor in low-priced stocks is greater than most other investment alternatives. Hundreds of slick opportunists understand this motivation and will often use this greed factor to promote virtually worthless securities through any means available. If you are involved in the market at all and utilize the Internet for trading or information purposes, there is no doubt that you have probably received innumerable unsolicited tout letters recommending various low-priced situations that they claim are about to explode in price sometime over the next few days or weeks. Don't be surprised if you get invited by these tout promoters to a cocktail party or dinner for presentations on this wonderful company they are representing to introduce you to this company that has tremendous prospects. If you receive one of these invitations and you happen to have nothing else to do at the time, go, enjoy the liquor and the food (usually they make the presentations in a nice restaurant or hotel), express your interest (it will make you feel less uncomfortable), and tell them you will think about it. But tell them, "Don't call me, I'll call you"; then, let them hold their breath. Unless you really want to make your money theirs, there is no need to feel guilty. These salesmen are usually cunning and ruthless and deserve absolutely no pity. If you got a meal out of them, consider yourself a hero. These types of presentations and seminars are no different than high-pressure condominium/vacation time-share sales. (At least if you wind up buying a condo time-share, you'll have your week in paradise once a year.)

Very often, the stocks that they are recommending are obscure, small, foreign-based companies with virtually no real or factual information available on them that would enable one to confirm or deny the outlandish statements their salesmen are usually making. In these types of situations, you are in fact getting bull rather than facts.

Very often, the salesmen touting these stocks have been handsomely compensated for their efforts by receiving large blocks of stock in these worthless companies. The motivation is to get them up in price so they can distribute this worthless paper to the unsuspecting, gullible dream chasers who figure, "Why not take a shot for a couple of thousand bucks?" In my 40 years' experience, and from my recollections, I have never seen or heard of any small touted so-called penny stock that turned out to be a real financial success. Yes, some of these stocks have gone up in price for short periods of time because of the effectiveness of the penny-stock promoters, but virtually none of them maintain their elevated prices for any significant period of time.

One of the reasons that these hyped penny stocks could never attain an investment value is that, in almost all these situations, the underlying business is fake. When I say fake, I mean the companies are a façade for the promoters to point to so they can embellish their business prospects to the targeted investor. Very often, the business of the company that is being used in these types of penny stock scams is usually trendy and currently being talked about in the media. For example, when the mainstream financial world is excited over biotech, you will very often see small, penny-stock biotech companies come out of the woodwork. When commodities are hot, numerous penny-stock mining companies proliferate. When China is in the news, dozens of penny-stock Chinese upstarts are typically touted by various promoters. In the late 1990s, hundreds of worthless Internet companies were not only brought public, but many were touted by unscrupulous promoters who took advantage of the public's insatiable appetite for anything related to dot-com investing.

Despite the SEC's supposed effort to rein in rampant penny-stock abuse, the proliferation of penny-stock promoters continues unabated. As a matter of fact, the techniques and practices of these promoters have become more sophisticated and effective than ever. Currently, besides the usual promotions found in bulletin board, pink sheet, and some small-cap Nasdaq stocks, we now have scams and promotions originating out of London (LSE), Germany, and most other countries that have trading venues. Often, promoters will go overseas to take advantage of the lax market regulations that prevail in some of these smaller, financially less sophisticated countries, which are just relatively beginning to embrace speculative capitalism. One way or another, penny-stock promoters will figure out ways to circumvent any new regulations that supposedly come out to hinder their business. It is important that the investor be aware of the realities that exist in this murky playground.

> ### Take Note
>
> One way or another, penny-stock promoters will figure out ways to circumvent any new regulations that come out that might hinder their business. It is important that the investor be aware of the realities that exist in this murky playground.

It is amazing to me how many of these tout sheets and market letters can penetrate the spam guards on my computer and wind up in my inbox. It is a testimonial to the determination of the unscrupulous penny-stock promoters who use all the traditional touting techniques, in addition to high-tech techniques, to get their message of greed in your face. The stories they present are very often convincing and tempting, but always remember: very few people who are not part of the scheme will ever see a profit from these scams.

Remember, as I mentioned earlier, LPVSs are virtually never touted or promoted by anyone. Therefore, if an alleged LPVS is being touted or recommended to you by someone with whom you are unfamiliar, the best decision would be to thank him very much and tell him to buy it for his grandmother. That will usually set him straight and he will seek another sucker to promote. You will do your homework, get the complete information on your target situation, and make your investment decisions based on facts.

> ### Take Note
>
> If an alleged LPVS is being touted or recommended to you by some-one with whom you are unfamiliar, the best decision would be to thank them very much and tell them to buy it for their grandmother.

Discovering the Undiscovered

Your job and objective as an LPVS investor is to sort through all the hype and rhetoric and attempt to discover a real undiscovered trea-sure. In order to accomplish this task, you must arm yourself with enough information and facts to distinguish between the hype and the substance. Obtaining correct and reliable information about an investment candidate, until just a few years ago, was an enormous effort requiring innumerable hours of work just attempting to ob-tain the necessary data. I can't tell you how many hours I spent at various libraries and regulatory information centers (Securities and Exchange Commission [SEC], National Association of Securities Dealers [NASD], etc.), trying to accumulate pertinent data on a po-tential LPVS investment candidate. Most of the work was manual and painstakingly slow. The data was often stale or missing from the file, and dealing with the bureaucrats was no pleasure at all. This was the historical way of "doing your homework"; the task of discovery and finding great LPVS candidates (buried treasure) was tedious, slow, frustrating, and often fruitless.

Still, if the effort resulted in a good find, it could readily be worth many thousands of dollars or more. All things considered, it was well worth the extensive effort required to discover a good, worthwhile, forgotten, undervalued, low-priced value stock situation. Perhaps the effort required years ago kept the LPVS opportunities more ex-clusive, by keeping the necessary data not as readily available to the masses as it is today.

Today, hunting for the buried Wall Street treasure in LPVSs is far less burdensome than it was in the past. Today's electronic access to a plethora of financial information sources is unprecedented in history. By simply making a few keystrokes on your computer, you can have access to all types of historic and current market information on just about any publicly traded security—information so complete and accurate as to be almost unbelievable, and in many cases access to this data is *free*. There are numerous entities offering these data services (some free while others charge various fees), which can readily answer most of your initial inquiries on just about any stock you want to be informed about. This makes performing your initial research effort on a potential LPVS almost a piece of cake, especially when you think about how much effort it took in years gone by. The immense amount of fully disclosed information available on these various sites can give you what you need to know when determining if a low-priced situation meets your basic criteria (listed in Chapter 2) and is worth the effort and/or investment. Remember, these sites will give you the information you'll need on a fundamental level but may not help you read between the lines or give much insight as to a company's real prospects and potential. Any site that gives you "advice" as opposed to the "facts" must be viewed differently than a pure information service. Take advantage of all the electronic data that is currently available when digging through the vast amounts of potential LPVS opportunities.

Take Note

Take advantage of all the electronic data currently available when digging through the vast amounts of potential LPVS opportunities.

The first part of doing your homework is to somehow generate ideas as to which of the many thousands of stocks traded really have the basic criteria to qualify them as truly undervalued low-priced investment candidates. As mentioned earlier, there are most likely numerous opportunities available all around you in the ordinary activities in your life. You may or may not think about them as opportunities because they may be too close to you and, therefore, you don't even see them or acknowledge their existence. Try to start observing things more in a businesslike fashion, and you may very well find a hidden treasure right under your nose. Great, small, undiscovered businesses, some of which are publicly traded, can be found all over our country and even internationally.

Realistically, most of you won't be able to find these situations in an efficient and timely fashion and would be better off exploring and searching for good LPVS candidates in a more conventional way. Today, the most efficient way to check out large amounts of potential LPVSs is to use one of the electronic sorting and scanning systems, which can quickly scan, sort, and identify securities based on your own personal criteria. These systems are updated in a timely manner and can be a great help in finding a potential LPVS based on a number of financial, price, trading, and industry criteria. A good scanning program, such as the software available at VectorVest.com, scans and monitors approximately 15,000 stocks and can be enormously helpful in helping you to identify interesting candidates based on criteria that you decide will work for you. Remember, if you make the criteria too stringent, you may very well not find any qualifying candidates; conversely, if you make them too loose, you may be inundated with potential possibilities. As you play with the system, you should be able to find a happy medium.

BigCharts.com (a MarketWatch service) gives the investor the ability to scan over 20,000 stocks by categories such as industry, performance, price, competition, and a variety of other criteria. The amount of data available is overwhelming, and this service can make your exploration far more effective and efficient. The basic service is free, with only small fees for premium services. The sites mentioned are but two of many that can guide, inform, and point out interesting LPVS candidates and steer any potential treasure hunter through the huge jungle of financial information. The candidates garnered from using scanning and sorting systems will provide potential candidates based on your selected criteria; this is a good start, but it is only the beginning. More pertinent information may very well be needed, which often will require hands-on review.

In my opinion, the best free web site (perhaps even the best among pay sites) and the one I personally use the most is the Yahoo!

Finance site. Information-wise, you can get just about anything, everything, and then some at http://finance.yahoo.com. The site is so good that I would be willing to pay for it, if the alternative were losing it. Once you have a potential candidate for consideration, this financial site can provide you with virtually all the information necessary to determine your selection's suitability as an interesting LPVS. Just about any publicly disseminated information can be found through the many features of this web site. To follow, you will see some of the criteria readily displayed, which can certainly help you confirm or refute your LPVS candidate's potential viability as an investment target. What Yahoo! can't give you is the ability to read between the lines, that is, the ability to see things in the facts presented that might convince you there is far more there than meets the eye. Experience will ultimately be your best teacher in being able to gain insight as to which factors, when combined, add up to a big potential winner. The other thing Yahoo! Finance can't do for you is to call the company (your potential candidate), speak with the management, and get a feel for what might be going on. Even this task is made easier by Yahoo! because the telephone number of the company and their business address is displayed alongside their web site address for your convenience. Remember, with few exceptions for premium services (at the time of this writing), it's *free*.

Take Note

Experience will ultimately be your best teacher in being able to gain insight as to which factors, when combined, add up to a big potential winner.

Hunting for Treasure

If you go to the Yahoo! Finance home page, it is very easy to call up a ticker symbol on just about any company (you can easily look up the ticker symbol if you don't know it). You will almost immediately see detailed, current stock-trading information. On the company's stock quote page under Summary (see Figure 3.1), you can find recent

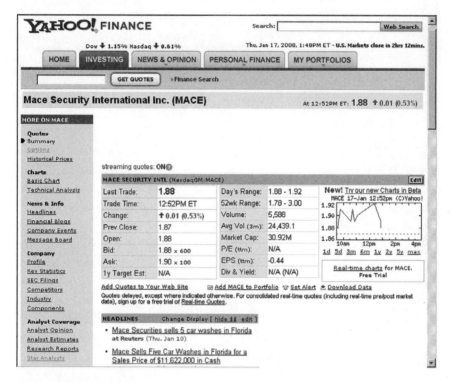

Figure 3.1 Summary

Reproduced with permission of Yahoo! Inc.® 2007 by Yahoo! Inc. YAHOO! and
the YAHOO! logo are trademarks of Yahoo! Inc.

news articles about the particular company and stock. This is very
valuable when you are trying to find out why your chosen stock is up
or down a significant amount. On this same page you will get a
sampling of much other pertinent information including current
pricing and volume (slightly delayed), basic statistical information,
a chart, and a menu for all the other features available. This page
is updated frequently, and the information is quite current and
accurate.

The menu of services found on the Summary page brings you to
specific areas of information and interest. Under the Headlines
section (see Figure 3.2), news articles from a variety of sources are
readily displayed in a time and date order; thus, it is very easy to
read about current news events affecting the stock. News articles
(and archives of past articles) appear for a company whenever that

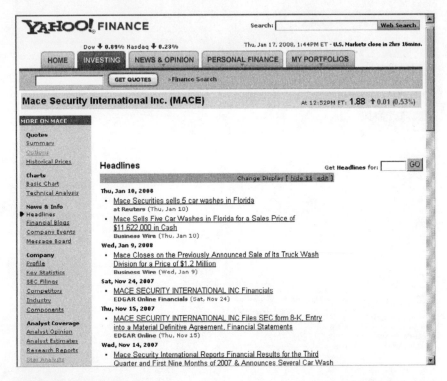

Figure 3.2 Headlines

Reproduced with permission of Yahoo! Inc.® by Yahoo! Inc. YAHOO! and the
YAHOO! logo are trademarks of Yahoo! Inc.

company's name appears in the article (it doesn't matter if the
company is the main subject of the article or not). The Headlines
section conveniently delivers all the news on most stocks going back
at least one year.

After you have entered a stock symbol, you then have access to
an additional large wealth of information. For instance, you can select Profile (see Figure 3.3) to get a good background report on a
company's business and some of its major financial numbers and statistics. This area also lists the company's top management and their
remuneration (a good thing to know). Another nice feature when
researching a stock is that on the Profile page there are usually links
to the company's own web site, and usually a link to the company's
own section for investors.

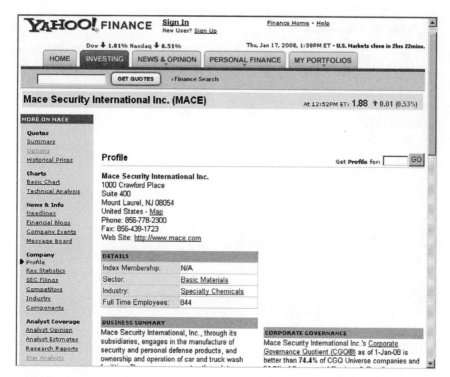

Figure 3.3 Profile

Reproduced with permission of Yahoo! Inc.® 2007 by Yahoo! Inc. YAHOO! and the YAHOO! logo are trademarks of Yahoo! Inc.

Perhaps the single most informative section of Yahoo! Finance is the Key Statistics segment of the site (see Figure 3.4). This section details just about every relevant financial statistic concerning your potential stock pick. It quickly summarizes over 60 different pieces of statistical information for your immediate consumption and perusal. Usually, this section can quickly give you enough information to either continue your analysis or sufficient cause to discard the candidate.

In the Analyst Opinion section (see Figure 3.5), one can learn about how many analysts are ranking the stock from 1 (Strong Buy) through 5 (Strong Sell). You can also see how the company has done in past earning announcements as well as expected future earnings. There also is a link to a page that contains information about which

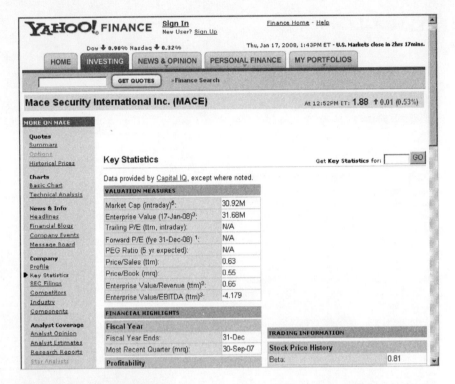

Figure 3.4 Key Statistics

Reproduced with permission of Yahoo! Inc.® 2007 by Yahoo! Inc. YAHOO! and the YAHOO! logo are trademarks of Yahoo! Inc.

brokerage firms cover the particular stock. The main reason an LPVS investor would look at this section would be to find out if there are *any* analysts following a particular LPVS candidate and, if so, how many. As stated earlier, a good LPVS is often an overlooked and forgotten stock situation with little or no analyst coverage. By reviewing this section, you will see if there is any real Wall Street interest in these shares and, if so, who they are and what they think. You may also be able to contact these analysts, speak with them, and develop further insight into the situation. Remember, be careful with much of this information and opinions; sometimes too much information can be detrimental to your wealth.

Another section that I find very useful is the SEC Filings section (see Figure 3.6). From here, an investor can get the information

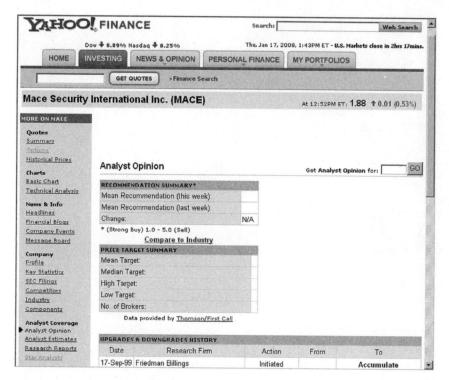

Figure 3.5 Analyst Opinion
Reproduced with permission of Yahoo! Inc.® 2007 by Yahoo! Inc. YAHOO! and
the YAHOO! logo are trademarks of Yahoo! Inc.

Take Note

A good LPVS is often an overlooked and forgotten stock situation with
little or no analyst coverage.

that the company files with the SEC, such as quarterly and annual
reports, substantive news events, meaningful business developments,
changes in officers and directors, and any other definitive material
agreements. This is a great resource to learn the official facts that are
filed with the top securities regulatory authority and thereby discover
more about the ins and outs of a company without the typical news
media slant and bias.

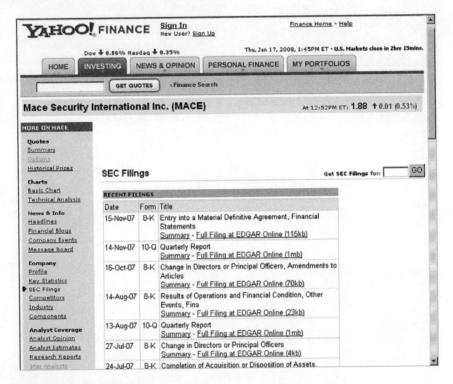

Figure 3.6 SEC Filings

Reproduced with permission of Yahoo! Inc.® 2007 by Yahoo! Inc. YAHOO! and
the YAHOO! logo are trademarks of Yahoo! Inc.

Insider Transactions is one of the most helpful sections to many
LPVS investors (see Figure 3.7). In this section, you can see what
stock transactions the insiders, large holders, executives, and/or
members of the board of the company have made. Following the
actions of the insiders can very often tip you off to the ultimate direction the company's stock is going to move. Unusual buying or selling
by the insiders, especially in LPVS securities, will often tip you off
that something is going on.

An interesting feature and a very popular feature that allows
interactive dialogue on Yahoo! Finance is the Yahoo! Message Board
(see Figure 3.8). Yahoo! maintains a message board/chat arena for
most individual stocks listed on most venues. While I would
never decide to buy or sell a stock solely based on messages posted
on these boards, some of the messages are informative and thought

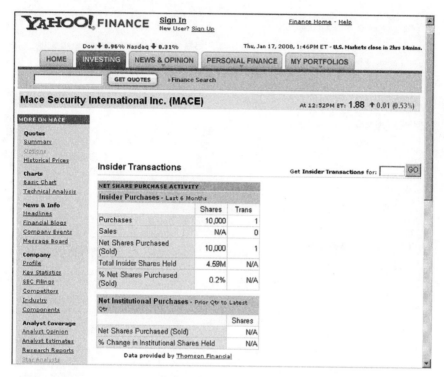

Figure 3.7 Insider Transactions

Reproduced with permission of Yahoo! Inc.® 2007 by Yahoo! Inc. YAHOO! and
the YAHOO! logo are trademarks of Yahoo! Inc.

provoking and may help you think about a company's potential.
However, you will find a lot of meaningless hype like "This stock will
go up 5 points by the end of the day": wishful, nonsensical chitchat.
However, a nice thing is that if you have questions about a company
that you are having a hard time finding out about, there is a good
chance someone on the message board might be able to steer you in
the right direction.

A wonderful feature that allows a potential LPVS investor to
quickly check out the recent price and trading action in the LPVS
candidate is a feature called Historical Prices (see Figure 3.9). Here,
in a matter of a few minutes, you can review the trading activity in
detail for just about any publicly traded stock. This review can swiftly
inform you if you are getting in at relatively attractive levels relative
to the recent trading activity. While exact pricing may or may not be

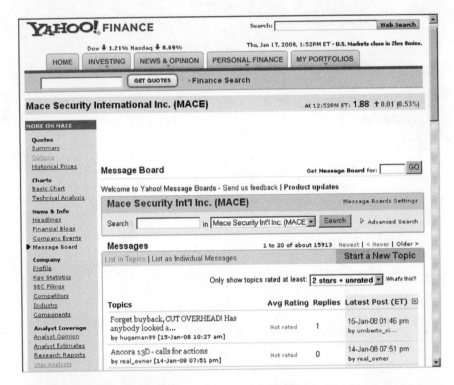

Figure 3.8 Message Board

Reproduced with permission of Yahoo! Inc.® 2007 by Yahoo! Inc. YAHOO! and the YAHOO! logo are trademarks of Yahoo! Inc.

relevant, it is interesting to see if the stock was significantly higher or lower in the past few weeks, months, or years. It will also demonstrate whether these shares really qualify as a forgotten and/or ignored situation. Years ago, a price search like this could have taken many hours of tedious labor.

A major determining factor in whether an interesting potential LPVS candidate should ultimately be accumulated is very often whether "smart money" (informed investors) is or has been accumulating the shares of your LPVS target. Yahoo! assists you in easily finding this information by simply going to the Major Holdings (see Figure 3.10) section of the Yahoo! Finance web site. This site will list the holdings of entities that hold meaningful positions of shares in the company. Obviously, if it appears that apparently

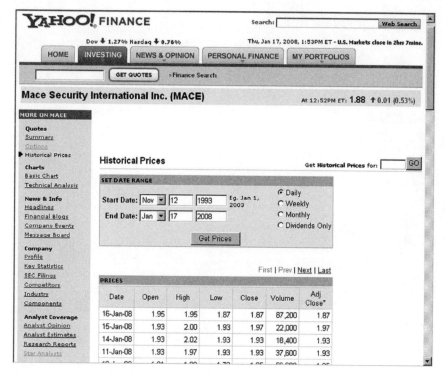

Figure 3.9 Historical Prices

Reproduced with permission of Yahoo! Inc.® 2007 by Yahoo! Inc. YAHOO! and
the YAHOO! logo are trademarks of Yahoo! Inc.

informed investors have been accumulating significant amounts of
shares, there is a better than even chance that they may be aware of
more information than the average guy. While this isn't always the
case, the odds are historically in your favor. A quick perusal of this
section may prove invaluable to your search for treasure.

One of the most often used sections on the Yahoo! Finance site
is and always will be Charts (see Figure 3.11), an area where graphic
charts are available. Yahoo! offers in-depth charts on virtually every
stock in its system. These charts give you at a glance the trading
history of the LPVS candidates for as short a period as a day or as
long a period as the company's trading history. The charts can be
customized to allow comparisons between companies and provides
split and dividend data on the companies.

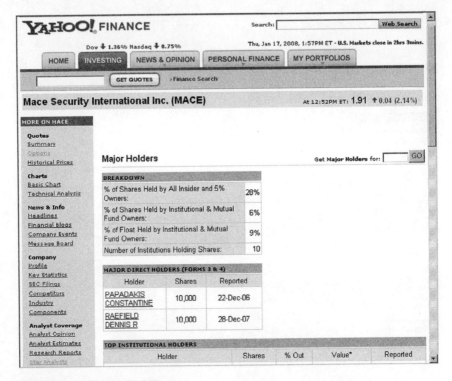

Figure 3.10 Major Holdings

Reproduced with permission of Yahoo! Inc.® 2007 by Yahoo! Inc. YAHOO! and the YAHOO! logo are trademarks of Yahoo! Inc.

Concluding Thoughts

There are many other features on the Yahoo! site that may or may not assist you further in your primary goal, which is to find and unearth the obscure and hidden companies that are very often just waiting to be discovered. Utilizing these tools on Yahoo! or some of the other market information sites allows you to cover far more ground in your LPVS treasure hunting than doing it the old-fashioned way. Just as a metal detector can assist avid beachcombers in their quest to find valuables hidden in the sand, a good market information system goes a long way in helping the avid LPVS investor in their quest to discover Wall Street's buried treasures. The only problem is that these information systems are available to all and

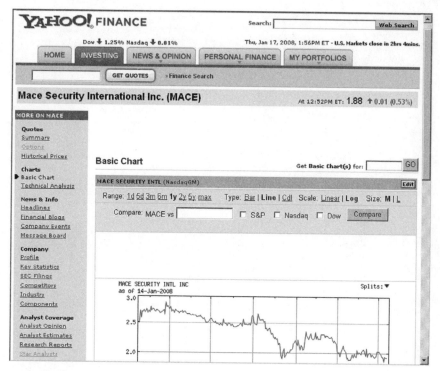

Figure 3.11 Charts

therefore the arena for competition is far greater than it was some years ago. The readily available market information can and will be used by more and more market participants creating a potentially more crowded playing field. As always, the more astute person will usually be able to prevail if they follow the outline I am divulging here.

Take Note

Just as a metal detector can assist avid beachcombers in their quest to find valuables hidden in the sand, a good market information system goes a long way in helping the avid LPVS investor in their quest to discover Wall Street's buried treasures.

CHAPTER 4

Public Shells and Reverse Splits, Options, and Warrants

When a company goes out of business and its shares were publicly traded, the shares are drawn down to the low-priced/penny-stock range because of this business reality. Some companies in apparent financial peril do not necessarily have to go bankrupt, but instead just choose to close their doors, often because they have run out of money and believe they cannot continue as a going concern. Many companies never had the opportunity to get too far into debt (no one would extend enough credit to them to begin with), and therefore no creditor has a large enough bad debt to undertake the time and effort necessary to force a bankruptcy proceeding on the company. These companies often did not have enough credit or assets to justify anyone's forcing them into a chapter, so the company just stops doing whatever business they were conducting and becomes dormant. Technically, the company still exists but they usually conduct little, if any, business. Many public companies have experienced this fate. Despite the fact that the company is dormant, its shares might very well continue to be quoted indefinitely. Usually, the shares of companies in this state are called "shells" or public shells. They usually trade in pennies or fractions thereof and have no real value, unless an interested party is seeking a public vehicle for an entity they want to become publicly traded.

Public Shells

When investing in any low-priced value stock (LPVS), including a potentially attractive public shell, you must be careful to analyze the total debt outstanding the company has because many companies that become potential LPVSs were at one time or another able to borrow heavily for their business. If the amount of debt that they accumulated during the good times of their business is high, it may be a sign that they will not be able to sidestep. In other words, if a company got too heavily in debt, it is more likely the company encountered problems in its business and the creditors went after the assets of a corporation when the company went into default. If the creditors go after the company's assets in the event of a default, often any value their shares may have had in a potential recovery, reversal, or reorganization may not occur because the debt would come first. The common stockholders in a reorganization may be totally wiped out of any value their shares may have had—permanently.

Public shells have recently been in demand by various parties who want their privately held businesses to become publicly traded. Many potential shell company acquirers are companies that have good prospects but have been unable to go public over the past few years because of unfavorable market conditions. Underwriters in many cases have been unable to raise money and take companies public because of the beating they gave the public in the 1990s when they sold them billions of dollars' worth of trash. This basic distrust of Wall Street underwriters is well deserved, and the public is reluctant to get burnt again. Therefore, many companies that desire to attain a public status seek out "clean" public shells with which to merge. By reverse merging with a public shell, the privately held company goes public through the back door. The advantages of being public are numerous, but there are also several disadvantages.

Being public gives a formerly private company public visibility and a quoted value. It provides liquidity for its investors and sometimes enables the company to raise new capital through private investment based on a stated public value. There are also tax, estate planning, and other potential advantages that can be gained by being public. Some shells may offer tax loss benefits to a merger partner, which can mean hard dollar savings to the newly formed entity if the merger is structured properly. If market conditions improve, the company can attempt to have an underwriter do a secondary offering and raise additional funds based on the currently trading stock price.

The disadvantages of being public are that the company is now accountable to many public stockholders who have the right to question, watch, and comment on its performance. The public company has accounting standards that must be met and in many cases has to comply with the Sarbanes-Oxley Act and many other regulatory obligations and requirements. Based on many circumstances and events, the price of this new publicly traded entity may or may not *please* the owners. All in all, many companies, after considering the pros and cons, still prefer to go the public route.

The desire to get public via a shell gives many forgotten low-priced/penny stocks a new lease on life. If a decent company is merged into an existing public shell, the shares held by the public may once again come back from the abyss and attain some reasonable value. The only reason I discuss this scenario is that when you do speculate in low-priced issues, some of them will most likely not work out on a fundamental basis and these shares might become for all practical purposes worthless, at least for period of time. However, on occasion, a company's value as a shell may very well revive life into the dead body of this formerly failed company. A private company seeking public status may very well want to acquire or merge with a public shell and pay a price to do it. Today, a clean shell can be worth almost a million dollars to a company seeking the benefits of being publicly held.

A clean shell is one with no outstanding liabilities or judgments, a reasonably small public float, a currently quoted market price, no pending regulatory problems, and other custom characteristics that may appeal to a particular acquirer (i.e., cash, tax loss carry-forwards). If an entity is willing to pay this price, it is very possible they are prepared to do something substantive with the newly merged company and make the old shares have value once again. Usually, the entity acquiring the shell will receive a very large amount of newly issued shares and thereby obtain majority control while diluting your original ownership percentage dramatically.

Nevertheless, a small piece of something good is a lot better than a larger piece of nothing. Where there's life, there's hope and perhaps ultimately a higher stock price. However, it might just be some promoters looking to make a quick buck by promoting and driving up the shares with the intent of dumping them on the public. In any event, as an owner you very well might get a second chance to recoup all or part of your formerly failed investment and in fact even make a good profit. Your low entry price made this possibility a potential reality. Examples of the above reemerging shell scenario will be given in a moment.

Reverse Splits

As you can see, there are many good reasons for one to expand their investment criteria into the world of quality low-priced stocks. The large profit potential relative to potential risk is, in my mind, the most compelling reason. Like all things in life there is always a catch or at least a large obstacle to overcome in any outstanding opportunity. In the case of low-priced investing, it is knowing which companies are truly high-probability winning candidates and which are the garbage penny stocks just waiting to lighten your load (of cash). Your ability to distinguish between the two will determine your success or failure. The next few chapters will describe examples of my thought processes and homework I used in sorting through, identifying, and picking winners in the world of low-priced/penny stocks. In addition, I will try to describe the trading techniques I employed to be able to accumulate major positions in some thinly traded low-priced stocks without moving the market in a way that would make the opportunities vanish. Great ideas that cannot be acted upon seldom become great realities.

Take Note

Your ability to *distinguish between companies* that have true low-priced value stock potential and those that are really just garbage penny stocks waiting to lighten your load will determine your success or failure in LPVS investing.

In the past few years, I have noticed a new reality in LPVS investing. Often, when the price of an LPVS stock drops below a dollar and the Nasdaq in their infinite wisdom threatens to delist it from their National Market section, some companies decide to "reverse split" their shares in order to raise the price to comply with Nasdaq's price rule. A reverse split is a procedure whereby a company divides the number of shares, it has outstanding by a factor to reduce numerically the number of shares, thereby proportionately raising the share price. For example, if a company has 10 million shares outstanding and the shares are trading at $0.50, it could then reverse split the shares by a factor of 10. The result would be that the company would now have only 1 million shares outstanding and all things being equal the shares would trade at $5. At $5 per share the company would once again comply with Nasdaq's ridiculous rule and remain listed on the prestigious Nasdaq National Market.

Take Note

A reverse split is a procedure whereby a company divides the number of shares it has outstanding by a factor to reduce numerically the number of shares, thereby proportionately raising the share price.

This new phenomenon I am noticing is that this reverse split, which usually was considered bearish, is now in fact helping turn the price action on several LPVS upward rather than further downward, as was the traditional belief. I believe there are several reasons for this reality. The fact is that at the higher price some institutional money can return to the shares. The significantly reduced float gives a scarcity factor to the shares. Many investors are turned off by small companies having many millions of shares outstanding. With a tighter capitalization, many investors including myself are more interested in taking positions in these companies. The continued Nasdaq listing appeals to some investors. A larger investor can buy or sell a larger portion of the company when forced to deal with market makers who all too often love to trade 100 share lots. On the Nasdaq National Market, a dealer must trade but 100 shares to honor their market whether the company has 1 million shares outstanding or 10 billion shares outstanding—ridiculous but true. These factors and others have had a positive affect on some forced reverse split stocks. To fear a reverse split is no longer valid.

As an example, after trading up to over $165 a share in March 2000, Priceline.com (PCLN) traded down to approximately $1 per share in early 2003, before management decided to reverse split the stock 1:6 (one for six) in June of that year. The newly split shares traded around the $6 level for a short period of time, then began a major advance in price after the reverse split. Within a few months, the shares of the reversed split stock traded up to just under $40 a share. By late 2007 the shares of Priceline had risen to over $110, a remarkable gain but only *after* the reverse split was completed. Another example of a reverse split's working out extraordinarily well was MicroStrategy Inc. (MSTR), a stock that collapsed from over $330 per share to $0.40 in 2002. After being reverse split 1:10 (1 for 10), the stock began a monumental rise back up to over $100 a share (late 2007 over $133). That's the equivalent of a $4 stock's rising to well over $130, but still nowhere near its split adjusted all-time high of $3,300 a share.

The reality is that many beaten-down stocks are still very good companies with good futures ahead of them. The reverse split tightens up the situation by bringing the price up to a more "respectable" level in the eyes of large investors and once again makes them suitable for accumulation. This phenomenon can very often give beaten-down, forgotten stocks the ability to once again regain their stature in the investment world.

Options

The people who are fascinated by the profit potential in LPVS investing may be tempted to dabble in securities that may be similarly priced and possess similar profit potential but in fact are totally different. While a good LPVS offers significant upside potential over a period of time, other types of securities may appear to have the same ultimate potential but can often offer this potential in a far shorter period of time. Tremendous profit potential, far more quickly than most LPVS investments, is the enticement of speculating in the various types of options and warrants readily available in today's market.

Options and warrants offer the investor/speculator the ability to take a small sum of money and potentially garner large gains in a relatively short period of time. The value of the option or warrant fluctuates based on the price movement in the underlying stock that the option/warrant represents. Before I go into detail on how the options and warrants work, remember these instruments are unlike LPVSs primarily because they have a fixed time limit attached to them. These instruments all have expiration dates attached to them and if the underlying stock does not attain a necessary price, the option/warrant may very well become worthless with absolutely no hope of recovery. This time limit and expiration feature is the main reason I do not recommend meaningfully capital commitments in option/warrant speculation.

Take Note

Options and warrants offer the investor/speculator the ability to take a small sum of money and potentially garner large gains in a relatively short period of time.

It is hard enough to pick a good investment opportunity without having to deal with a clock ticking on when exactly you will be right. Options are usually short term in nature, while warrants on balance have longer expirations. From experience, I can say that there is always too little time when holding options and all too many seemingly great option opportunities die due to lack of adequate time. When buying options or warrants, time is your enemy. For that reason and that reason alone, I would advise any potential LPVS investor to stay away from option speculation; timing is just too difficult to deal with. At least in LPVS investing, the clock is not ticking and you have whatever time necessary for your situation to work out (if ever). While potential profits in options speculation can be significant, all too often the speculator winds up watching their entire investment disappear when the options expire worthless. Options and LPVS investing/speculation, despite the pricing and upside potential similarities, are vastly different creatures and must be treated as such. Options may initially appear to be potentially more rewarding over a shorter period of time, but my experience tells me you will make far more money picking good LPVSs in the longer run with far fewer sleepless nights.

> ## Take Note
>
> When buying options or warrants, time is your enemy.

To be fair, a few details and characteristics of options and warrants seem in order. I do not encourage low-priced option speculation, but understanding what they are about is a good idea. This text is not meant to be a guide to options, but the following information about these often low-priced securities can come in handy when the temptation comes to place a large "bet" on a stock.

Option Contracts

Option contracts give a purchaser the right to buy or sell a security, such as stocks, at a fixed price within a specific period of time. Calls and puts are the two most common options. Call options enable you to purchase a stock at the strike price at any time before the expiration date, while puts allow you to sell a stock at the strike price at any time before the expiration date. An option in itself has no intrinsic value other than the right to buy or sell at the strike price until the expiration date; afterwards, if not exercised, it becomes worthless, carrying no value. An option gives the buyer a right and the seller an obligation; therefore, the buyer who received something of value must pay the seller (writer) a fee called an option premium. For the option purchaser (also called the holder), an option offers the right but imposes no obligation to buy (call option) or sell (put option) a specific quantity, usually 100 shares per contract, of a given stock at an agreed-upon price (strike price), until the call (expiration) date, in exchange for a premium (option price).

A market participant who believes that a stock's price will rise might buy a call option, the right to purchase the stock, rather than just buying the stock itself. He would then have no obligation to buy the stock, only the ability to do so until the expiration date. If the stock price increased over the exercise price by more than the premium paid, he would profit. However, if the stock price declined, he would let the call contract expire valueless, and only drop the amount of the premium. A trader may possibly buy the option instead of shares, because for the same amount of money, he could acquire a larger number of options than shares. If the stock rises, he would then pull off a larger gain than if he had purchased shares, and that is where the rub is. The temptation to invest the same amount in the options as in the stock itself creates a scenario in which, if the stock drops even a small amount during the option time period, the options may very well go out worthless—a 100 percent loss of investment. If the trader had bought the underlying shares instead, his investment would be diminished to a greater or lesser extent while an aggressive option strategy would usually cost him his entire capital commitment in the options. Unfortunately, the nature of a treasure hunter is all too often to go for the gold and try to strike it rich—quickly. This trait may very well spell disaster for an LPVS investor turned option speculator. Don't do it!

Writing (selling) a call option while owning the stock is called covered call writing, while naked call writing refers to the practice of selling calls without owning the underlying shares. Many call the latter a very risky strategy, because the price of the underlying stock could shoot up without limit, leaving one no choice but to buy the underlying stock (or call) back at a large loss. A trader who thinks that a stock price will decline can sell short the stock or, alternatively, sell a call. Either tactic is risky and generally never appropriate for smaller individual investors. The player selling a call has an obligation to sell the underlying stock to the call buyer at the buyer's option. If the stock price diminishes, the short call position will turn a profit to the extent of the premium. If the stock price rises over the exercise price by an amount greater than the premium, the short will lose money, by a potentially *unlimited* amount.

There are a wide variety of options strategies that can be employed through the use of put and call options. This text is not nearly detailed enough to give you the background or advice you would need to enter the field of options straddling, so, for informational purposes only, I will discuss a few.

Take Note

A trader who thinks that a stock price will decline can sell short the stock or, alternatively, sell a call. Either tactic is risky and generally never appropriate for smaller individual investors.

Covered Call Writing.   A covered call involves acquiring an underlying stock and selling call options against it. If you believe the market will be relatively flat and remain in a narrow trading range, sell a corresponding call and generate premium, which reduces your entire position's break-even price. You earn additional income from your stock by writing slightly out-of-the-money calls regularly (monthly, quarterly, etc.). As writer of the call, if the stock remains range-bound, upon expiration, you get to keep the entire proceeds of the option premium(s). You make money even as your shares stagnate. If the underlying stock declines in value by more than the call premiums received, you will lose money. Alternatively, if the stock goes up above the strike price of the call option, you will most likely have your shares *called* and you will, in fact, be obligated to sell them. At that point, you can let that happen and take your premium profit, or you can preserve your upside potential in the stock by buying back the stock or the same call you originally sold (before it was exercised) in the open market.

In summary, if the underlying stock rises, calls are exercised and your stock is sold at the strike price. If the stock stagnates in price, the calls will probably expire worthless and you will earn your premium and continue holding the shares. On the downside, you will earn your premium upon option expiration and continue holding your shares—for better or worse.

Uncovered Call Writing.   When you write uncovered (or naked) calls, you sell a call option without actually owning the underlying shares. In this case, while your maximum upside is limited to the premium you sell, your maximum loss is unlimited (the underlying stock of the option you write could go ever higher, keeping you on the hook for what is in theory an unlimited loss). If you are indeed called away, you will be forced to hand over shares you don't own at the prevailing market price. Call buyers see limited risk in exchange for the possibility of unlimited upside, while naked-call writers take on unlimited risk for only limited profit potential. Naked-call writing is the riskiest option strategy around, so much so that brokerage firms require that interested investors meet stringent margin and capital requirements. My advice: tread lightly—or not at all.

There are numerous strategies that utilize both long and short put and call options in all sorts of combinations. These options strategies allow traders to profit from volatile, range-bound, or even stagnant stock market scenarios. Some of the more notable options strategies are called straddles and strangles, along with a variety of "spread" strategies commonly known as bull and bear call, butterfly, ratio, vertical, box spreads, and so on. All of these spreads combine put and/or call options with various strike prices and expirations in a variety of ratios, which attempt to accomplish the desired market results. As indicated earlier, *I do not recommend the average investor to go anywhere near this environment* without advisers of the highest caliber, and, even then, I would try my hardest to get the urge out of my system.

Warrants

As I emphasized earlier, options in general are not a suitable investment choice for the LPVS player. Aside from the all-too-present risk, the biggest negative is investing against the clock. It is certainly hard enough just being right as to market direction. When you compound that difficulty by putting in time parameters, in my experience, you are really making it unduly difficult to make money. There is, however, an option-like investment opportunity that, by its nature, may be suitable for an LPVS investor's mentality. What I am talking about are warrants, option-like securities that mirror standard equity options in many ways, with the primary difference being a much longer exercise period.

Take Note

A warrant is an option-like security that mirrors standard equity options in many ways, with the primary difference being a much longer exercise period.

Warrants are very similar to call options, and often bestow the same rights as an equity option to the investor. They are also traded in secondary markets. However, warrants have several key differences.

A warrant's expiration period (life) is usually measured in years (as much as 15 years), while options expire in only months. By comparison, LEAPS (long-term equity anticipation securities), the longest-term stock options offered, expire in no more than two or three years. As in options, upon expiration, warrants become worthless unless exercised due to the underlying stock's being higher than the strike price of the warrant.

- Warrants, as options, are subject to time decay, but it's not as pronounced an issue. Time value diminishes as time goes by—the rate of decay increases as you approach the date of expiration.
- Warrants are issued by private entities, most often the corporation on which a warrant is based.
- Warrants issued by the company can be dilutive.
- Warrants do not have voting rights.
- Warrants typically do not trade as actively as listed options and often as an over-the-counter security.
- Warrants are not standardized and may contain certain features or restrictions not typically found in more widely traded exchange-listed options.

For purposes of the LPVS investor, the key difference, the one that makes certain warrants acceptable as a potential LPVS candidate, is the potentially long expiration periods they might possess. By having several years left in their life, the warrant takes on the characteristics of the underlying stock without the impending danger of nearby expiration risk. Naturally, at some point, time decay expiration risk will come into play; however, that may very well be years from now. With adequate time, warrants represent the same ownership potential as the underlying stock, with a lower capital outlay and thereby ultimately lower economic risk (same characteristics as options but for a far longer period of time). The fact that so much remaining time exists is reassuring for the investor because it gives the situation the time necessary to work out.

Of course, the reason for buying a good warrant must be the same as the reasoning for buying any good low-priced value security. The proper warrant can make a higher-priced value candidate take on the characteristics and benefits of lower-priced value stocks by reducing the amount of the financial commitment to the investment. The fewer dollars put at risk in terms of price, the greater the potential percentage gain in the event of a price increase in the underlying stock. Also, if the underlying stock declines in value and your warrant is low enough in price and premium, it should not go down as much as the stock itself. A well-priced long-term warrant is a superior way of in fact owning a stock; however, the most important reason to own the warrant is that you believe you are correct in investing in the underlying stock. Do not allow a warrant that seems attractively priced to convince you to make the investment unless you also believe the company is a worthy LPVS investment.

Take Note

A well-priced long-term warrant is a superior way of in fact owning a stock; however, the most important reason to own the warrant is that you believe you are correct in investing in the underlying stock.

CHAPTER **5**

Overcoming the Obstacles

Investor, Be on Your Toes

I have been critical of the Wall Street establishment for years, so much so that some might think I have a vendetta or paranoid hatred for the investment community. Well, I would say that I am paranoid, and with good reason! When I see an organized attempt by some of the most powerful and respected people in our society to systematically fleece the investing masses out of the money they often kill themselves to earn, it ticks me off. I have not forgotten the fleecing of America in the Internet fiasco at the beginning of the millennium. Millions of people's pension funds were depleted, while slick Wall Street businessmen bought major league ball clubs and personal jets. People denied themselves a few extra dollars so they could invest a little extra in their future in a mutual fund, while the fat-cat money managers let their friends trade, virtually risklessly, against the fund after hours. Major accounting firms—the protectors of the public's interest—were all too willing to bend the investing public over for a big scoop of consulting dollars. Major Wall Street firms systematically orchestrated sophisticated schemes to fatten their wallets in massive initial public offering (IPO) frauds. Large corporations committed so many scams I can't even begin to enumerate them. And all this nonsense was going on under the watchful eye of our supposedly efficient regulatory organizations.

My conclusion is that it is almost impossible to prosper in a market when these types of conditions are allowed to exist. While much lip service has been paid to some of the atrocities committed by the financial community, little can and will be done to prevent these scams from happening over and over again. The price paid by perpetrators who commit or aid in committing financial fraud or other securities law violations is seldom severe enough to deter offenders. Perpetrators of crimes against the investing public are unlikely to get caught. Regulators in general are interested only in high-profile corporate criminals, the type of securities law violators that will put a feather in the cap of an aspiring bureaucrat looking to make a name for themselves. The smaller corporate criminals seem to be the primary target of regulators when they need an easier target to go after. Larger corporate criminals usually have deeper pockets and can fight back more effectively.

Even if a regulator comes down hard on a corporate violator, the investor virtually never comes away unscathed and always remains a victim of the fraud. Despite major lawsuits filed by innumerable law firms and the varying degrees of success they attain, seldom do investors realize even a small portion of the loss they incurred by the perpetrator's fraud. Prison sentences are seldom issued, and even when they are, the term is inconsequential relative to the size of the dollar amounts lost or the devastating impact caused to the victims. My conclusion is that investors should insulate themselves as much as possible from conventional, mainstream Wall Street. The positives of your interactions, if any, aren't worth the hurt they are more than willing to dish out.

Take Note

Investors should insulate themselves as much as possible from conventional, mainstream Wall Street. The positives of your interactions, if any, aren't worth the hurt they are more than willing to dish out.

Simply put, following mainstream Wall Street's advice is a surefire way to get nowhere. The risk you take to get ahead of the game is not justified by the rewards, if any. The advice spewed by the high-priced analysts and market specialists can be nothing short of crap. Conventional wisdom is often the wisdom created by the powers that be, who usually have their own agenda. As I have taught my students for years, a trade represents a difference of opinion. One side buys while the other side sells (the ultimate difference of opinion!). Who is right and who is wrong? Do I know more about the situation than the contrary side, or am I being led like a lamb to slaughter? Keep in mind that mainstream Wall Street's advice is suspect at best and is usually well disseminated by the time you get it.

Take Note

A trade ultimately represents a difference of opinion. One side of the trade buys while the other side of the trade sells.

LPVSs: A Sensible Option?

Is the low-priced value stock (LPVS) an answer to the crowd mentality of Wall Street? Absolutely, in my opinion! As discussed previously, I have earned returns on LPVSs so much higher than conventional securities that, for me, there is virtually no comparison. Of course, I have had losers, but on balance the winners can be so significant that they can easily eliminate the pain of the losers. Well-picked LPVSs have given me returns of several thousand percent on several occasions, while the biggest loss I have ever taken on a losing pick has been a maximum of 100 percent of the money invested in that particular issue. Even if the number of losing selections is greater than the number of winners, the ultimate returns can be quite impressive.

If you follow the logic presented in this book, you no doubt can see the potentially large returns one can obtain from a successful portfolio of LPVSs. What I haven't gone into yet is how one finds, identifies, and qualifies a good candidate for accumulation and investment. This is the $64,000 question, perhaps even a lot more. Remember, the LPVSs we are looking for seldom have anyone telling you about them or following them with the intention of informing you. If someone does point out a low-priced stock, most people believe—and rightly so—that it is probably a penny-stock tout and are skeptical, suspicious, or worse. Early on in my career, when telling a friend about an LPVS I was buying, he replied in a strong tone, "If it's so good, why don't you buy it yourself?" Despite the fact that he was and still is arrogant, he made a good point. If I found an unknown, undiscovered, unfollowed, undervalued gem (the definition of an LPVS), why on God's Earth would I want to tell anyone? I should just accumulate the shares to my own financial ability and reap the rewards. Sooner or later, if my logic were correct, the market would discover this undervalued gem and the price of my shares would rise precipitously.

I believe strongly that true value will eventually be discovered by the market and be reflected in higher share prices. Conversely, stocks trading on hype and stories will ultimately become worthless. I have a little saying that I've used to describe this phenomenon for years. It's a bit graphic, but it clearly gets the point across: "Cream always rises to the surface, while sh** eventually falls to the bottom of the bowl." I think these are words to live by!

Knowing—Half the Battle

For years I have kept my LPVS investing techniques to myself and discussed them only with a few close friends and associates. Opening up these ideas and techniques to others could just turn these potential huge opportunities into thinly traded overly volatile situations. The point is that capitalizing on LPVSs requires an entirely different strategy of investing: research and techniques not usually employed in conventional investing.

In conventional investing, accumulating a position in a mainstream stock can take but a few seconds. If I chose to buy a $100,000 position in JPM, GE, DIS, or WMT, it would take me but a few seconds to buy the shares. A simple click of a computer key completes the task. If one wanted to take a similar position in an LPVS, it could take a much longer period and much greater care. Accumulation of the desired shares can take extended periods of time and must be accomplished with a "sealed mouth" strategy. If word gets out that a meaningful buyer is accumulating shares, the entire opportunity may be nullified by a rapid reappraisal of the company by other opportunistic traders, market makers, or investors. Various trading techniques must be utilized to disguise your intentions if you expect to accumulate your position at the desired price. Until the proliferation of direct access trading apparatus became widely available to the general public, many of the suggested methods of accumulating thinly traded LPVSs would have been virtually impossible. The minute you placed an order for the shares, the entire street would be aware of your desires, and unless there were large natural sellers of the shares you desired, all you would probably accomplish is running up the price of your targeted buy and nullify this opportunity. You must know what you are doing before entering the market to buy or sell thinly traded securities. I will discuss basic techniques later on.

Years ago, a very famous Wall Street personality told me repeatedly, "If you want a friend on Wall Street, buy a dog." What he meant was that nobody working or connected with the financial arena is your friend; they are merely people interested in profiting in whatever way they can from an association with you. While some may say this is a very cynical view of Wall Street, I have come to learn that it is true and probably a very understated observation. My personal observations are far harsher. I believe that virtually every aspect of our financial community, especially Wall Street, is or has been corrupt. I don't take this statement lightly but make it only after being a student, observer, participant, and hopeful reformer of the market for over 40 years. Fortunately, some areas are getting better after the embarrassment of scandal after scandal, but, overall, many abuses by Wall Street and its related parties still exist. Just recently, the subprime mortgage scandal was exposed. This scandal will adversely affect perhaps millions of people, including homeowners, investors, and innumerable related parties for years to come, and this is another "gem" perpetrated by said Wall Street crooks in their three-piece suits and wing-tip shoes. Go figure. (See Figure 5.1.)

Knowing that your chance of getting a fair shake on Wall Street is almost an impossible dream, investors must arm themselves with strategies and initiatives that will protect them in their journey of investing. One might wonder why anyone would want to venture into the market at all, considering the many ways Wall Street abuses the

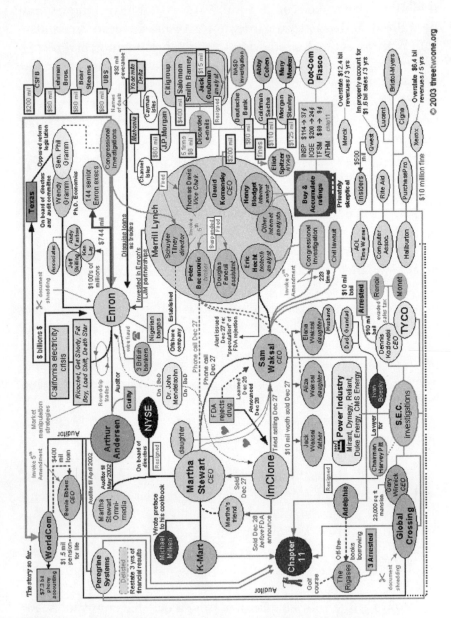

Figure 5.1 Major Wall Street Scandals of the New Millennium

Source: Threetwoone.org.

public customer and even the pro. The answer is that investment returns on "safe" investment alternatives are basically unacceptable. Inflation, which is certainly rearing its ugly head, requires one to do something to stay whole, much less get ahead. Bank accounts, money market funds, certificates of deposit (CDs), and other guaranteed-type investment products have yields today that are so low they don't return enough to outpace even today's low inflation rate. What this means is that in real terms you lose spending power by saving in these conservative alternatives. Most people want to at least keep up with inflation and earn a net positive return. Lately, this has been quite difficult because rates are down, inflation is up, and making money in the market has been extraordinarily difficult.

Take Note

You lose spending power by saving in conservative alternatives like bank accounts, money market funds, certificates of deposit, and other guaranteed-type investment products because they have yields today that don't return enough to outpace even today's low inflation rate.

Conventional wisdom of the past just doesn't seem to hold water in today's fast-paced, computerized world. Companies today are finding it harder and harder to survive and prosper in today's highly competitive international and domestic markets. The "buy-and-hold" strategies of the past are no longer valid in most cases today. The media spews out so much rhetoric on so many venues, people no longer know what to believe or how to interpret the massive amounts of data. Yet life goes on, and the reality is that one must attempt to get ahead of the game somehow. Usually, that means taking some kind of action that entails various degrees of risk.

The action I am suggesting to you, though, is based on a premise you are not likely to hear anywhere else. Take a portion of your risk investment dollars and put them into high-value, low-priced stocks. If you do this, I believe the returns over time could dramatically exceed the returns earned in conventional investing strategies.

Overcoming Obstacles

Accomplishing one's objectives in successful LPVS investing is an endeavor that requires a concerted effort, not unlike virtually every other type of market participation. Identifying potential candidates, researching all the various criteria for selection, picking an attractive industry or group, and then making the decision to commit capital to your choice are tasks that should be fulfilled in any type of investment activity, not just LPVS investing. However, there are other obstacles that one must overcome when dealing in LPVSs that are not usually prevalent in more conventional equity investment and speculation. Perhaps the most notable is learning how to effectively trade in and out of thinly traded stocks.

Take Note

Identifying potential candidates, researching all the various criteria for selection, picking an attractive industry or group, and then making the decision to commit capital to your choice are tasks that should be fulfilled in any type of investment activity, not just LPVS investing.

Thinly Traded Stocks

While most equity investment positions can be established by simply entering a buy order for the security in the amount desired, many very desirable LPVSs are often thinly traded and the accumulation (buying) or distribution (selling) of these shares can be a bit more problematic. Very often, a relatively small number of shares either bought or sold can cause significant price movement in both directions. While most investors love to see the price of their shares rise quickly, that is only the case after you already own the shares. If you are in the process of buying the stock, rapidly rising prices on small amounts of volume can mean you are paying too much or not accumulating the stock at all. Knowing how to properly work your order can surely help you establish the position you desire at the appropriate price.

Counting on a broker to properly execute your orders in LPVSs often will prove very disappointing, as the brokerage community makes a good deal of their income off the backs of investors, their customers. Routinely, brokerage firms direct their orders to "friendly" market makers and dealers for execution. While small orders in actively traded securities usually get executed relatively quickly and fairly (true only in the past few years due to electronic execution and new Securities and Exchange Commission [SEC] regulation), orders for larger amounts of more thinly traded stocks can be an opportunity for abuse that few market makers can ignore or resist. The thin nature of these stocks can allow a market maker to quickly run up the market price abnormally in order to enable them to fill the client's market order at an extremely elevated price. Once filled, the market maker can simply allow the stock to settle back to its former level and thereby replace the shares he sold, hopefully for a nice profit. The same phenomenon is true on sell-side transactions. While it may appear to be only pennies in the pricing, as a percentage, these pennies are market-maker "perks" that can often cost an investor large sums in lost profit or even actual losses.

The best way to overcome the structural disadvantages of trading your desired stocks is to eliminate the brokers and dealers to the greatest extent possible. Remember the old adage, "Brokers make you broker"; when value investing in low-priced stocks that are usually thinly traded, this saying is very true. Your best choice is to open an account with a brokerage firm offering a "direct access" trading platform that will allow you to enter your orders directly into the market through an electronic communications network (ECN). These firms provide a front-end software package that allows you to monitor virtually every U.S. stock on the various exchanges and enter orders by simply pressing a few buttons. These orders interact within the market instantaneously and can assure that your order cannot and will not be ignored or traded around/through. While these direct access systems are not yet perfect, compared to just a few years ago, executing orders through them is relatively fair and efficient, far ahead of any conventional execution technique. Subjecting yourself to the old way of market interaction, through a conventional broker, could be considered the height of stupidity!

For years, I have repeatedly told every student, client, and friend, "Wall Street is not your friend." Every aspect of Wall Street is designed to extract as much money from you as possible. From the brokers, market makers, research analysts, and back-office operations to corporate finance, all the operations are designed as profit centers. If you look at the recent earning reports from the major brokerages, you will see that they are quite good at what they do—so beware.

Take Note

Every aspect of Wall Street is designed to extract as much money from you as possible. From the brokers, market makers, research analysts, and back-office operations to corporate finance, all are designed as profit centers.

Patience Is a(n Investing) Virtue (and So Is Silence)

Another obstacle that must be overcome when LPVS investing is the desire to jump the gun. After you think you have uncovered and discovered the right candidate, the usual desire is to establish your position ASAP. This, however, may not always be a good idea or even possible, especially if good executions (fills) are desired. Being in a hurry usually can be very costly and in many cases can actually harm your objectives by helping to distort the very market you are attempting to interact in. I suggest that you open your position by buying a small amount of your total proposed position at the market (maybe 10 percent) in order to establish a starting point. Hopefully, this small purchase will not disrupt the quoted market. Then, I would begin, through an ECN, to bid for small amounts of the shares, by placing bids alongside the other market makers at the current high bid price. If the shares begin to come in on the bid, remain at that price until you feel you have purchased enough at that level; then reduce your bid as necessary until you have purchased the number of shares desired.

If, however, after a reasonable period of time, your bid is not hit (accepted), you may choose to raise it slightly (a cent or so) or if the shares are offered up a penny you may decide to "take" the offer (buy the shares offered up a cent) up to the amount desired. If this process enables you to buy your desired number of shares, good. If not, you can repeat the above upticking, but do not get carried away and drive up the price of the stock on yourself. Be patient; often, it takes a little time for sellers to realize that their stock is trading at higher levels, and therefore there may be time delays until the sellers place their sell orders that may very well satiate your appetite for the shares. Naturally, the reverse of the above trading scenario is basically true when liquidating (selling) your position. If there is nothing going on (little or no trading) in the shares of your targeted choice, there should be little need to be too aggressive—you should be able to accomplish your objectives in an orderly and efficient fashion without attracting undue interference.

Remember, while attempting to accumulate or dispose of your position, *keep your mouth closed!* The fewer people who know what you are doing, the greater the probability of getting your objectives accomplished. Market makers are not your friends, and in these situations even your friends are not your friends. As they said during both world wars, "Loose Lips Sink Ships." The fewer people who are aware of your buying (or selling), especially in these thinly traded stocks, the better. Once you have purchased (or sold) your desired amount, then feel free to talk if you feel the need. Remember, you're the one who did the research and work, so you deserve the opportunity of being first among your peers to interact in the market. Being first certainly doesn't necessarily mean you're going to be right, but you deserve the opportunity to be first. There are plenty of others out there who may in fact know more than you and/or have far deeper pockets—you may not be right with your pick.

The reality is that when you are involved with a position, especially an LPVS, there will often be significant price fluctuations. Relatively small market orders in these shares can lift or drop the quoted price in the shares by large amounts percentage-wise. A $0.10 drop in a $1 stock is a 10 percent move, which is quite significant to a person with a sizable holding (everything is relative). The emotions, fear, panic, uncertainty, greed, and others are always factors that investors must deal with. In thinly traded LPVSs, the emotional factors are even more intense than investments in larger, more well-known blue chips. People seem to understand and/or accept when a widely held large-capitalized stock moves up or down significantly, but a sizable move in an LPVS seems to be much more nerve-racking. Does one step in and buy more into a decline or sell out to "save their home"? These realities are perhaps one of the greatest obstacles one must face when dabbling in the more obscure, unknown LPVS world.

The urge to take small profits in LPVS investing can be very significant. The temptation to take a few pennies in profit, which can readily be justified by the size of the percentage move, must be rationally dealt with. For example, if an LPVS you have purchased at $0.50 rises suddenly to $0.60, one may be very tempted to take the $0.10 profit by selling their position. This $0.10 profit represents a 20 percent gain, and that is an amount that can take four to five years or more to earn in a savings account or CD. While I can't fault a person for ever taking a profit (you'll never go broke taking profits), the objective of investing in LPVSs is to earn returns far beyond conventional offerings. To accept just small returns on an LPVS may be, in fact, shortchanging yourself. Accepting all the risks of LPVS investing, participating, and then walking away too early from a good pick will often drive one crazy.

Overcoming this dilemma is possible. I have found that occasionally trading against my LPVS position can keep my emotional needs in check while satisfying my need to take profits, yet retain my position until a more opportune time comes to cash in. Remember, an LPVS should be held until it no longer qualifies as an LPVS. At a high enough price, its elevated price may make it only a fair-, neutral-, or even overpriced security and no longer desirable as an undervalued speculation. What price is it when an LPVS is no longer viewed as low priced or a value stock? That is a question for the ages. Since no one knows for sure, that is why I consistently trade against my LPVS holdings in an attempt to generate some current profits while waiting for an optimum time to distribute the larger portion of my position, hopefully at significantly higher levels.

The trading of the LPVS shares on a regular basis can keep your emotions under control while you patiently wait for the home run you hope is coming. If you are successful at occasionally buying the dips and selling the blips, you may very well keep your emotions in check and make yourself nice trading returns while waiting for your ship to come in. The conquest of boredom is what a reasonable amount of trading can accomplish, and boredom is an obstacle that must be overcome in order to succeed.

Take Note

What price is it when an LPVS is no longer viewed as low priced or a value stock? Since no one knows for sure, I consistently trade against my LPVS holdings in an attempt to generate profits while waiting for an optimum time to distribute the larger portion of my position, hopefully at a higher level.

Keep Some Powder Dry

Always keep in mind that, when their time arrives, LPVSs will usually move very quickly in percentage terms—so quickly, in fact, most investors will not be able to react fast enough. What this means is that you must have a position in place if you expect to prosper off an anticipated move. You will not often be able to interact immediately during the rise. Even if your LPVS pick drifts down a significant amount over a period of time, it may take only a few trading minutes to recoup a significant amount; that is the nature of LPVS situations. Do not expect a good low-priced value stock to trade like a more widely held, higher-capitalized market situation.

No matter how much you may believe your LPVS selection is on target, the current price is ridiculously low, and an excellent time for accumulation exists, always realize it could well go lower in price before hopefully making its rise. As many pros are well aware, today's lows may be tomorrow's highs. Picking bottoms (as well as tops) is almost impossible, and for that reason, one should always "keep some powder dry." A pirate would understand this expression, but for those of you not familiar with cannons, it means to have some firepower remaining at all times. In the case of LPVS investing, it means keeping a little buying power available for those times when market aberrations may spike down your LPVS candidate to a level never contemplated or believed possible. The ability to "average in" more shares at seemingly unbelievable prices is a good position to be in, although according to conventional investing, averaging down is usually considered a no-no.

Concluding Thoughts

In LPVS investing, you are buying significant value (in your opinion) at hopefully very depressed prices—prices below tangible net worth and/or cash and marketable securities. Even if the price you paid for your opening position appeared very low, it is very conceivable it will trade even lower—it's the nature of the game. By keeping some powder dry, you can nibble on additional shares, if and when the opportunity presents itself. Remember, most LPVSs, due to their low price, are not marginable, meaning your brokerage firm will not allow you to borrow money against them to purchase additional shares (as in higher-priced listed securities). This means you will be required to have some cash reserves available from other sources in order to have buying power available when needed (dry powder). Always try to be in a position where you are never out of the game and prepared to move forward even if your holdings are at times lower in price.

All in all, while you may encounter some other obstacles from time to time, nothing should be so problematic that it will interfere with your overall objectives. The reality is that if you learn and understand what you are trying to accomplish, overcoming any obstacles in your way should prove readily achievable.

Take Note

Always try to be in a position where you are never out of the game and prepared to move forward even if your holdings are at times lower in price.

CHAPTER 6

Getting an Overview
of the Marketplace

In order to fully appreciate the concepts and theories that I am espousing in this text, it is vital that you understand the backdrop of the marketplace in which you will be interacting. The realities of investing in stocks and other securities are seldom fully understood by the masses. Many times, the average person enters into the Wall Street arena half-cocked and not fully aware of their ultimate objectives or the impediments they will encounter before ever achieving their goals, if they ever attain them at all. Surely, most investors, speculators, traders, and the like all want one thing: profits and gains. Unfortunately, these are not always the results of a venture into the Wall Street arena. As many times as not, the other side of the coin appears: losses and frustration.

As I said before, the basic premise of trading is the fact that when one person or entity is *buying*, another is *selling*—the ultimate difference of opinion. I must emphasize this fact repeatedly. By definition, your purchase of a security is being consummated by the directly contrary act of a seller, who may or may not be smarter or more sophisticated, informed, knowledgeable, and connected than you are. This reality shouldn't necessarily frighten you or scare you off, but if you are to survive and prosper in the Wall Street arena, you must always be aware of this difference of opinion and remain cognizant of the fact that others very well might know more than you do. With this realism always in the back of your mind, you can proceed and hopefully prosper.

> ### Take Note
>
> By definition, your purchase of a security is being consummated by a directly contrary act of a seller, who may or may not be smarter or more sophisticated, informed, knowledgeable, and connected than you are. Don't let this frighten you; just be aware of this difference in opinion.

A Little History

Getting ahead of the game by investing in the stock market has been an endeavor that has extended over 400 years. Stock in companies, representing fractional public ownership, began trading in the early 1600s in Holland. Back then, stocks were bought and sold by dealers in the city of Amsterdam, and their activity soon became known as an exchange—the Amsterdam Stock Exchange (Beurs)—where they began continuous trading on a regular basis. In the latter part of the seventeenth century, not to be denied, England picked up on this activity, and a stock exchange was formed in London. The Dutch established many types of new financial maneuverings never before utilized, including short selling and options trading, to name a few. From these beginnings, there are now stock markets in virtually every developed and most developing countries. The world's leading markets are now found in the United States, England, Japan, China, India, Germany, France, and Canada.

While virtually all the above markets welcome market participation, be careful before throwing your hat into the ring; it would be wise to have a good understanding of what you are getting involved in. An understanding and overview of the realities will determine your chances of success or failure and their extent. As I have indicated throughout this book, I believe the markets are very slanted toward the side of the market professionals and the Wall Street elite. These people have had a head start of hundreds of years and have used that advantage to develop a system that on balance gives them every edge conceivable over the average public investor. All the laws written to protect the average investor have been enacted in conjunction with the Wall Street elite and therefore usually contain nuances that keep the entrenched interests "large and in charge."

Only recently have a few laws been enacted giving the average investor better information and access to the public securities markets and, I am proud to say, I was instrumental in instigating some of this long overdue reform. Transparency and access are terms used by the regulators to describe the new more-beneficial features of today's market environment. Former head of the Securities and Exchange Commission (SEC), Arthur Levitt Jr., the twenty-fifth and longest-serving chairman of the United States Securities and Exchange Commission (1993–2001) was widely hailed as a champion of the individual investor. In his best-selling book, *Take on the Street* (New York: Pantheon, 2002), Levitt discussed his frustrations over not being able to reform the markets in a meaningful fashion. While I considered him to be by far the greatest market reformer of our time, it is apparent that even his efforts were far from enough to overcome the entrenched powerful interests of the financial services industry. Harvey Pitt, Arthur Levitt's successor (also a brilliant man), soon resigned his position as SEC head, apparently due to his frustration over his inability to instigate meaningful change. It is interesting to note that the finance and investments industry is one of the largest, if not the largest, contributors to the political scene in the United States, as well. Given these examples, it's no wonder why so little reform or change is instigated by our politicians on our sacred Wall Street.

With a Careful Eye

One must always look to cover his own back when committing his hard-earned capital to any investment. The reality is perpetrators of frauds and scams flourish in the financial markets with hardly a day passing that doesn't bring to the forefront another financial crime or atrocity. Knowing whom to trust or which information and disclosure are accurate can be a nerve-racking task. While our regulators try to give the appearance of doing their jobs adequately, the reality is that if they don't, and you become a victim of a fraud or scam, your hope for recovery is almost assuredly little to none. Perhaps eventually the perpetrators of the crime will do a little hard time, many years after the event, but your chance of recovering any of your lost investment is negligible, especially after the class-action lawyers get their hands on whatever is left of the decimated company. The old expression, "Let the buyer beware," is very true when making financial commitments in the Wall Street arena. All too often, people feel that our system of regulations and laws permit them to lower their guard, but I'm telling you—*don't do it!* Consider yourself on your own when investing in most Wall Street products. Stocks are not insured savings accounts and CDs, so if you invest in them, make sure the potential return is great enough to offset the risk that is inherent in all uninsured investments.

> **Take Note**
>
> Stocks are not insured savings accounts and CDs, so if you invest in them, make sure the potential return is great enough for you to offset the risk that is inherent in them.

Be Aware of the Media

The financial media, in my mind, has become quite problematic with respect to the average investor. Today's media has taken on an entertainment stance as opposed to being a news and information source. I am now often dismayed by programming on major financial information shows, which, in my opinion, try to make news rather than reporting it fairly and in an unbiased fashion. Beautiful women and men gasping in surprise in concern over a report of an earnings miss, which in many cases is an inconsequential event, can truly distort the actual event. The analyst that supposedly called the miss may in fact have an axe to grind, and calling it a "miss" to begin with may be a serious distortion. The producers of these shows are always looking for stories; after all, they have hours of airtime to fill, and a story is just what they need. It may be good show business, but it can be harmful to a naive public that all too often responds irrationally because of a theatrical presentation. Take a look at the after-hours market response to an earnings release that has been dramatically reported by the real-time financial media. Violent swings all too often occur for reasons that are soon reversed or modified when the dust is allowed to settle. In after-hours, a stock might be up or down significantly, but when the stock opens for trading the next day, the shares may be far less impacted. I personally believe the public is all-too-influenced by the tone and demeanor of the reporter disseminating the news event. I understand that the proliferation of active traders exasperates the reaction of reported news events; however, the media presentation of breaking news has a tremendous influence on the subsequent trading in a stock.

Take Note

Take a look at the after-hours market response to earnings released that day by dramatic reporting. Violent swings occur for reasons that are soon reversed or modified when the dust is allowed to settle.

Which news gets disseminated on the major media sources is also subject to whims of the source. Very seldom is the news of smaller companies followed by the major media sources unless it fits a story they are working on or there is little news elsewhere for them to report. The lack of media coverage on most small-, micro-, and nano-cap stocks could be a major reason why there are a good number of LPVS situations available for the treasure hunter. Seldom does any credible business news source run stories about a very small company unless something they are doing is timely in their eyes and worthy of public dissemination. Most good LPVSs have good businesses and prospects but may very well be too mundane for the overall media to get excited. These companies just run a good business, make profits, grow in an orderly fashion, and very often do not capture the media interest until they get noticed by a more sophisticated takeover artist who *discovers* what has been there for possibly a very long time. Don't look to the general media for good ideas when it comes to LPVSs; they have too many reasons for not following them until a "news" event brings them to the surface. For example, not long ago I presented a great LPVS situation to one of CNBC's most prominent commentators and was basically told the situation was "too small" to be disseminated openly by him. His impact on the shares could be overwhelming (at least temporarily); he preferred to *pass* due to this fact alone. Apparently, the media has its constraint.

Perhaps that is in fact good news for the value-seeking investor. If the media places the spotlight on a great LPVS, its status as an LPVS may soon be altered by the public media exposure because the low-price aspect of the LPVS may very quickly disappear, sometimes in a matter of seconds. As discussed earlier, with today's direct access and instantaneous media dissemination of information, rapid price movements are the rule, not the exception. Cheap stocks this minute may be relatively expensive literally minutes later—good news for the LPVS investor when the time is right.

> ### Take Note
>
> With today's direct access and instantaneous media dissemination of information, rapid price movements are the rule, not the exception. Cheap stocks this minute may be relatively expensive literally minutes later—good news for the LPVS investor when the time is right.

Overall, an extensive business media is a good thing for those of us who know how to accept and react to the mountains of financial information thrown at us daily. In general, listen, watch, and read what the media is disseminating, but carefully think about its real meaning before you go and chase the stock they are talking about (either up or down). I find that many of the initial moves tend to reverse and go back to the level they were before the media report. This is true because most things they report were well anticipated by the market pros or numerous other people in the know and the stock's pricing has already been reflected prior to the news event. How many times have you seen stocks go down on apparently good news and run up on what you might perceive as terrible breaking news? The media only delivers the news, but how it affects the market is still in the hands of the powerful market pros.

The media can sometimes make business deals either happen or not happen. The media's influence on public opinion can be instrumental in whether a deal takes place or not. For example, when Rupert Murdoch was attempting to buy the *Wall Street Journal,* many media sources were totally negative about his consummating this deal. Were the many reporters truly reporting the facts, or were they in reality pushing their own agenda with *spin,* fearing a consolidation of business media, which could have a negative affect on *their* jobs. A CNN commentator called him a "meddler" and indicated that the merger would be bad for the workers. Other prominent media sources branded him a "scorpion," "villain," and a "tyrannical dictator." All this negative media was designed to have the public perceive this deal as terrible and Murdoch as ominous, and that the deal shouldn't happen—in effect, attempting to make news rather than report it. In fact, the deal did take place and many people prospered substantially from its consummation. Remember, a reporter's take on the news they are reporting is of little importance to the actual happenings, and an astute investor will try to separate the facts from the opinion and hype. Most of what reporters say is coming off a teleprompter, the text of which was put together by a behind-the-scenes person—a producer, news clerk, or in some cases interns, who, many times, are unpaid college students. Take it for what it is worth before you act on it.

Be Aware of Market Volatility

There is more volatility in today's market than at any time in market history. Today, a 300- to 400-point move in the Dow Jones Industrial Average is not uncommon and almost expected from time to time. As recently as 2005, volatility in the U.S. markets was relatively low, yet today's wild swings seem common. Many technical analysts believe that volatility is considered a contrarian indicator; high readings are considered an oversold condition, while low readings are considered overbought. Historically, volatility measures often move inversely to the overall price trend of the major indices. Rising volatility often indicates an expectation of a declining market and can be a sign of lower prices. Falling volatility often accompanies rising markets and indicates a high probability of a bullish near-term outlook. These are only indications but can be used to help build supporting evidence of a price trend. The reality is that trends change and that trying to base investment decisions on volatility indexes is the equivalent of playing in traffic. As for the LPVS investor, they should care little as to these indicators and in general pay but slight attention to technical indicators when engaging in LPVS investment strategies.

Volatility is good for short-term traders, especially day traders or short swing traders. Rapid price fluctuations give a trader the opportunity to capitalize on short-term price movements. If you are willing to take the risk of super-short-term price volatility, your rewards could be awaiting, but always be aware that price volatility is a double-edged sword and the potential for loss is most assuredly always present. An LPVS player usually avoids the stress of volatile markets by being involved in stocks that often "trade by appointment," rather than chasing their tails with high fliers. Sometimes the LPVS trader may get bored with the slow movements, but it's a lot less painful than being on the wrong side of an unstoppable freight train. Truly evaluate your tolerance for risk before getting involved in high-volatility stock situations.

Take Note

Truly evaluate your tolerance for risk before getting involved in high-volatility stock situations.

Hedge Funds: Market Movers

From my perspective, it seems that market volatility has a great deal to do with the concentration of huge sums of money in the hands of a relatively few high-stakes money managers and hedge funds. A hedge fund is an investment fund structured to avoid direct regulation of activity and strategy by most authorities. Most hedge funds charge their clients a fee and have millions of dollars under management. In addition, they are not as regulated as other investment strategies. Investing in a hedge fund is usually considered more risky than other alternative investments, but expectations for higher returns are par for the course.

Because hedge fund activities are more limited, they use strategies like futures hedging, short selling, swaps, and so on, to leverage themselves more often than other investment strategies. And because they manage so much money, they have great influence over the market-place, whether they succeed or fail in gaining revenues. I, for one, be-lieve there should be more regulation of hedge fund activities—some sort of watchful eye—due to their overwhelming market influence.

Hedge funds usually charge 20 percent of gross profits as a per-formance fee, but this percentage can fluctuate widely, with some newer managers earning significantly less, while other, more-proven managers can receive even higher fees. For example, reportedly, Ste-ven A. Cohen of SAC Capital Partners, while not taking a manage-ment fee, receives a 50 percent incentive fee for his efforts; and Jim Harris Simons of Renaissance Technologies Corporation allegedly receives a 5 percent management fee and a 44 percent incentive fee from the Medallion Fund. Most managers find charging a perfor-mance fee incentivizes their managers to work harder for their in-vestors than a flat fee (that is paid out to the manager whether their accounts do well or not).

And, While We're at It, a Word on Commonality of Interest and Tacit Collusion

In my opinion, hedge fund arrangements to a great extent have been the cause of much of today's market volatility. As noted earlier, large hedge fund managers get paid their percentages on both the realized and the unrealized profits on their trading accounts. Therefore, if a large hedge fund has an enormous position in a particular security at the end of an accounting period, it might very well make sense for them to buy up some additional shares at this end point to try to dramatically increase the value of their position for "mark-to-mar-ket" purposes (the value for period-end accounting and payout pur-poses). This can have the effect of dramatically increasing the value of the portfolio and thereby significantly increase the payout to the fund manager. The vast sums under the control of various funds makes these interim markups very simple and a very profitable game for the money managers who receive their payouts, usually in cash. Ever won-der why so many hedge funds have huge positions in the very same stocks (GOOG, YHOO, AAPL, RIMM, etc.). Most times, trading these stocks to higher and higher levels, in my opinion, has little to do with their fundamentals but much more to do with "tacit collusion."

Tacit collusion occurs when cartels are illegal, and overt collusion is absent, when two or more firms agree to play a specific strategy without explicitly saying so. Since all these firms have the same vested interest in keeping these favored positions at higher and higher levels, they may have the incentive to tacitly collude by monitoring the movements and acting accordingly. I'm not saying this goes on, but it certainly has an aroma. This type of markup behavior can go on for extended periods with all colluders enjoying the ride. If the payoffs for colluding are greater than the penalties for cheating, then the participating firms will usually choose to collude (tacitly). If and when the market collapses, however, the investors in the fund can be severely burnt while the fund managers still keep their untold millions. The monumental collapse of the Internet stocks in 2000, in my humble opinion, to a great extent was a direct result of this type of tacit collusion among major funds.

To prevent the negative effects of tacit collusion and dissuade money managers from pumping up their holdings at the end of certain financial periods, in some instances, hedge funds have instituted a practice known as a high-water mark, where managers won't get their incentive unless they exceed a benchmark from previous years. It also goes to show that if a high-water mark is not in place, a manager could systematically draw down a fund's assets at the expense of its investors, depending on the system of bonus they are managed under.

The high-water mark does not always accomplish its goal because a manager who has lost a meaningful amount of capital may simply decide to close the fund and begin again with a fresh slate. Naturally, his investors would still have to want to continue with him. A lot of well-known market makers criticize these types of bonuses because they don't incentivize managers to look at the long haul and reap revenues for their clients for the long term. Only time will tell if the industry adopts a more fair and prudent approach to keeping their funds' and their managers' activities successful.

The realities discussed here must be fully understood in order to prevent investors from being taken advantage of by the moneyed players prevalent in today's market. My advice is to make every effort to stay away from their game, if possible, or, alternatively, try to understand it as much as possible and interact *with* the flow rather than against it.

7

A Classic Low-Priced Value Stock:
Sportsman's Guide (SGDE)

In the late 1990s my wife introduced me to David, the husband of a friend she had made at the spa where they both worked out. David and I hit it off immediately and soon became good friends. David is a successful attorney who would probably be described by most people who know him as a little weird, not because of his profession but, rather, his social quirks. His most unusual trait is his fascination with his armed forces past and his desire to express himself by wearing paramilitary garb as well as enjoying other military behavior and paraphernalia (training marching music, MREs [meals, ready to eat], combat boots, etc.). An intelligent and successful man, he was and still is very much an enigma.

You might ask why this is relevant to successful investing in today's market. When you understand how this man's unusual behavior played an integral part in leading me to one of my biggest scores ever on Wall Street, it will become very clear that great ideas can come from the most unusual places. As I stated earlier, great ideas seldom come from mainstream financial experts because of the many reasons described earlier. Great ideas often come from recognizing the obvious—things you can readily see and understand but are all too often afraid to act upon because you don't have the confidence to honestly think yourself capable, believing that only

Wall Street experts know what's right, especially in financial matters. Nothing could be further from the truth. I have found that many relatively intelligent people are often far more capable of making prudent investment decisions than the so-called Wall Street pros. Too many undisclosed factors and agendas skew the professional's opinions and advice.

Back to David and his military fetish. As friends, we hung out regularly with a few other guys (all professionals: a businessman, doctor, pharmacist) on the weekend and would go saling—not sailing, as on a boat, but rather garage sale(ing) in our local neighborhood. We usually didn't need anything we bought but rather accumulated mountains of miscellaneous junk just to see who could negotiate the best deal on a particular item or items. It became a bit of a competition, and the winner earned the privilege of paying for lunch. We all laughed our asses off and had great fun; an entertaining day was had by all. One Saturday morning when David picked me up to go saling, I noticed a cheaply printed catalog on the seat of his car. I asked what it was, and he proceeded to explain to me that it was a catalog from a company called Sportsman's Guide (see Figure 7.1). He went on to say that they had a great selection of military surplus "stuff" at great prices, as well as hunting, fishing, and all kinds of outdoor sporting goods at deep

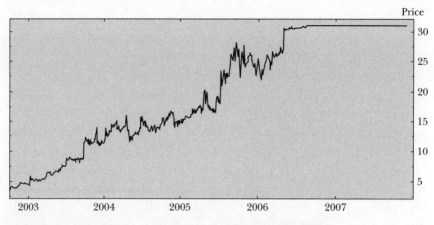

Figure 7.1 Sportsman's Guide Inc. (SGDE), 2003–2007

Data source: Yahoo! Finance, Nasdaq.com

discounted and closeout prices. As a matter of fact, they offered quite a good selection of various merchandise at incredibly low prices, including shoes, clothing, and other interesting products primarily for men. Being an avid bargain hunter, I immediately took notice, got their telephone number, and requested that the catalogs be sent to me pronto.

A New Investment Interest

I received my first catalog almost immediately, and others in various categories shortly thereafter. It seemed that they had several categories of merchandise and provided separate specialty catalog issues for each at various intervals during the year. They distributed literally tens of millions of these various catalogs every year to many thousands of customers. The many unique merchandise offerings were often compelling, and the pricing of the items was extremely competitive.

Gary Olen, the founder of the company and its spokesperson, wrote descriptions of the merchandise that were very informative. His style of writing was most entertaining, making reviewing the catalogs a real pleasure. Often, I would peruse the catalogs late at night when I couldn't sleep, find an interesting item (boat shoes, hunting knife, Swiss Army watch, two-way radios, etc.), pick up the phone, and order it on the spot anytime day or night. They were open 24 hours a day, 7 days a week, and had customer service people who were exceptionally competent, courteous, and friendly. It was a pleasure talking to them, and I routinely ordered more merchandise than I originally planned to because of the staff's tremendous upselling abilities. They also offered a buyer's club membership for $29.95, which gave members an approximate 10 percent discount on virtually everything they offered, as well as a first crack at certain limited closeout items and other special offers not necessarily available to nonmembers.

Overall, I found this company to be a pleasure to do business with. On every catalog they sent out was the typical necessary information about ordering, billing, delivery options, return policies, and the like, but also a little statement about the company, stating that Sportsman's Guide is a publicly traded company listed on Nasdaq under the symbol SGDE. Despite my extensive background on Wall Street, I gave this situation little thought, as upon a cursory review, the stock seemed fairly priced at the $7 to $8 level. Being a value player, I didn't see any compelling reason to own these shares at what I believed to be only a fair valuation. As stated earlier, I look for stocks that I believe to be cheap because of their overlooked status in the financial community. SGDE was being followed at the time by some on Wall Street, and it seemed to be trading in a neutral range, as far as I could tell.

Take Note

Look for stocks that are cheap because of their overlooked status in the financial community.

The Market Condition Changes

From time to time I would check out the price of the stock but had little investment interest in these shares. A small secondary offering of shares at the $7 level was issued by a California underwriter in 1999 to help facilitate its developing an online format for its catalog business. This was the time when Internet stocks were on fire and an irrational exuberance prevailed in reference to any stock that was associated with the Internet. The offering was completed, raising enough new capital to enable SGDE to commence the integration and development of the new web site for the Sportsman's Guide catalog operation. The development and implementation costs for this web site caused the company to lose a small amount of money and took a significant amount of time. Normally, these facts of business life would have been understood and accepted by the market gurus; however, this was in early 2000, the time when the Internet meltdown began to occur. Within a matter of weeks, any company associated with the Internet became persona non grata, and the geniuses in the financial community who were strongly recommending these shares with wild abandon suddenly developed amnesia. Anything associated with the Internet, had "Internet" in its name, or had even the slightest tinge of the Internet stench became instant garbage, and the shares of these companies were sold down to almost nothing.

Included in this group were the shares of Sportsman's Guide, which, through little or no fault of the company's management or game plan, was victimized by the Internet stock collapse. Within a matter of weeks the shares of SGDE were pounded down relentlessly from the $8 level to well under $1 by the end of 2000. There was absolutely no fundamental reason for this decline. Their plan to put the catalog on the Internet was proceeding nicely, and, in my opinion, at the time the only sure thing the Internet would probably be good for was an electronic catalog-like operation. The Internet catalog would at a minimum significantly reduce the printing and postage expense of distributing the catalogs, enable instantaneous updating of merchandise availability, and enable the accepting of orders electronically without the need for human beings. These advantages seemed obvious to me then in 2000, without even knowing at the time the innumerable other benefits and efficiencies of an Internet backbone.

While most other Internet companies had huge numbers of shares outstanding and market capitalizations that defied comprehension, SGDE had a very small number of shares outstanding. Many Internet companies were issuing stock as if it didn't matter, using the shares as an alternative currency for compensating employees and making often little-thought-out acquisitions at ungodly high prices, using massively overpriced stock to pay. For an Internet company to have issued hundreds of millions or even billions of shares was not unusual. This situation was perpetrated by the Wall Street analysts continually having "strong buy" ratings on these worthless pieces of crap and a financial institutional community often all too willing to buy these stocks blindly based on the advice and "deals" made to them by these Wall Street crooks. Naturally, the idiots who comprise all too many of the public investors jumped on these stocks with wild abandon, having dreams of the untold riches that would surely ensue. SGDE was an exception to this phenomenon. They had kept their capitalization very tight and had an issued and outstanding amount of shares totaling only about 4½ million shares, with little to no long-term debt. In the Internet arena, this type of situation was virtually unheard of. Despite these realities, the professionals on Wall Street pounded down the price of SGDE along with the majority of the other overhyped Internet stocks throughout the year 2000. By late 2000 the shares of SGDE, which had been trading over $8, had fallen down to the $0.60 level. The Internet debacle had created one of the best opportunities I had ever experienced in my investing history.

After analyzing this situation and putting my fears aside, I decided to start accumulating the shares of SGDE. Remember, the year 2000 had been a disaster for the stock market, especially the Internet environment. To commit any significant funds to any stock during this time period, especially something Internet related, seemed insane. However, going against the grain is the way most big money on Wall Street can be made, especially if you are confident in the underlying fundamentals of the investment. SGDE had already been relentlessly beaten down, there was little to no buy interest in the shares, the fundamental health of the company seemed all right, the potential for the success of the Internet web site appeared high, and all of the above met my criteria for a low-priced value stock (LPVS) investment. Understand that no one recommended this situation to me; I had no special information concerning this company, no whispers, no touts, no inside advice from people in management, just commonsense analysis based on my personal experience with this company and a basic perusal of the publicly disseminated information filed by the company. No magic or special advantage, just what I believed to be clear thinking.

I began my accumulation during tax selling in December 2000 when the shares dropped to around $0.60. I quickly accumulated about 25,000 to 50,000 shares at that level from the various market makers who traded in these shares, who were more than happy to sell them to an apparently crazy buyer. As I accumulated more shares, the frequency at which they were being offered and sold to me began to slow, so I began to gradually raise my bid for the shares. It makes absolutely no sense to pay up for shares when you are virtually the only one accumulating them; however, after tax selling ended, the flow of shares being sold at lower levels had essentially stopped. As I went up on the bid for the SGDE shares, an interesting phenomenon started to occur. The market-making community, which, in my opinion, had apparently shorted many of the shares I had purchased, rather than raising the price of the shares to hopefully be able to attract a real seller and buy back their short, decided instead to go to war with me. They began to offer and sell me more and more shares in the hope they could break the back of this stock. Often, this strategy worked, especially with the highly capitalized "crap" Internet stocks, which had been so heavily distributed to the public. However, this strategy, which appeared valid, based on the very weak Internet sector at the time, proved very wrong with SGDE.

The market-making community would sell me tens of thousands of shares every time I began to uptick the quote on the stock. The assault at times even had me second-guessing myself; after all, I was virtually alone in this accumulation of shares and often thought I might have been going too far out on a limb. Every time I had these reservations about my actions, I rethought the situation logically and reconfirmed my belief that I was correct and on the right track. I might have also muttered a little prayer. I was becoming more and more knowledgeable about this situation by calling the company, speaking with management about the progress of the new web site, overall financial conditions, and how the company was doing in its existing business. From the beginning, I was pleased with management and believed they had things under control, they appeared very competent and their agenda was well thought out. I also knew through years of experience that most market makers can't chew gum and tie their shoes at the same time, so I was not really concerned that their aggressive selling was based on any heavy thought or factual analysis.

Take Note

If you have a large stake in a company, don't hesitate to call them up and speak with management about the progress of the business and the overall financial conditions.

Making Decisions on Your Own

During this period, I met an interesting professor of finance at a National Association of Securities Dealers (NASD) seminar that was held at my former alma mater, Baruch College. He was a learned man who taught financial and stock analysis at a prominent Midwest university. We became somewhat friendly, and I retained him to write an analytical piece about SGDE just to confirm my opinion of this situation. I told him to be brutally honest, as this work was not to sell or influence me, but rather to confirm or refute my opinion. It took him a couple of weeks to do his analysis, and he wrote up his unbiased opinion of SGDE based on classic fundamental, standard, academic analysis. His opinion was that there were better retail stocks out there to buy, including Amazon and other conventional retailers with Internet ambitions. After reading his piece, I believed more than ever that I was right and he was dead wrong. That's what makes up Wall Street: differences of opinion. Every time a stock trades, it means there was a difference of opinion; one side thinks it's a buy, while the other side thinks it's a sale, thereby creating a trade. As it turned out, his analysis was based on the company's past performance, with little insight as to the probable future prospects for the company—20/20 hindsight. Thank goodness I decided to totally ignore his report.

I continued to buy shares relatively aggressively despite this report and the market makers' continuous attempts to draw the price down. As I gradually raised my bid on the stock price higher and higher, approaching the $1 level and even higher, the battle became more intense. This battle enabled me to acquire several hundred thousand shares over a period of several months. Considering the fact that there were only 4½ million shares in total outstanding and the majority were held by corporate insiders, this large accumulation in a narrow range, near the low end of its historic trading range, in the open market, was quite impressive, to my way of thinking.

Establishing a Position

As stated earlier, having a great idea about a potential LPVS investment and actually making it come to fruition are two separate tasks. There are times when a great idea can quickly disappear if the price of an LPVS quickly rises before any meaningful accumulation can be made. Bidding up the shares too quickly without being able to buy a meaningful amount sometimes nullifies the idea itself. This is especially true in very micro-cap stock situations. Remember, there are people who do know, or should know, the value of a stock (management, accountants, lawyers, employees, etc.,) and can, or will, usually step in if they notice large accumulations away from themselves, especially if they are in a position to do so. In larger-capitalized companies, accumulating a position is not nearly as difficult for the average or even larger investor. Usually, the market for higher-cap stocks is easier to maneuver in, even if they are considered LPVSs. The widespread holdings of the shares by numerous investors usually allow for significant differences of opinion, and therefore accumulation of a meaningful position can be relatively easily achieved. One must know the number of shares an LPVS has outstanding, the number of holders who control those shares, and the makeup of the shareholders. With an understanding of this information, one can determine how to approach the market when trying to establish a position. Naturally, I am addressing the investor who is prepared to commit a sizable amount of capital in a particular situation. For those of you who play smaller, accumulating your shares should not be nearly as difficult, although many times market makers will run up a stock on even small orders if they think they can beat you out of even a few extra cents. Try to work your own orders through an electronic communications network (ECN) or a direct-access platform when possible. This will make it more difficult for brokers and market makers to take advantage of you.

Take Note

One must know the number of shares an LPVS has outstanding, the number of holders who control those shares, and the makeup of the shareholders. With an understanding of this information, one can determine how to approach the market when trying to establish a position.

After I established what I believed to be a relatively significant position, I continued to monitor the stock for the next few months. Slowly but surely, the company proceeded to develop its business plan on schedule and constantly improved its operations. The number of buyer's club memberships continued to increase on a steady basis, and the introduction of the web site showed immediate results. These fundamental successes kept a floor on the stock all through 2001 when the market really took a dump, highlighted by the 9/11 disaster in September 2001. The tragedy of 9/11 did not hurt SGDE or its shares, and it even turned out to be a windfall for the company. SGDE inventoried and sold a great deal of army surplus paraphernalia, and as you might recall, gas masks and other related military-type terrorist preparatory merchandise suddenly became in big demand. Although this phenomenon didn't have a material impact on the company's sales or earnings, it immediately became a company to be looked at and monitored. It suddenly hit the radar of the financial community, and that's what it takes to get out of the ignored and forgotten category to the "let's take a look" mode. Once the investment community started showing a little interest in this situation and in conjunction with an outstanding financial track record of growth and profitability, it was uphill from there.

At the time I was accumulating the shares of SGDE, there was but one financial services company working with the company, which was charged with being their public relations adviser. The firm Bluefire Associates out of Minneapolis was a small firm that apparently advised the company on various public relations issues and other corporate topics. One day I called the representative at Bluefire to hear what they were saying about the company and discuss what was happening at SGDE. During our conversation, which was going along very positively, I asked who the larger holders of the stock were. He answered by saying there were three or four sizable holders of the shares. I proceeded to ask if he felt that any of them would be willing to sell their shares at or around current levels. I suggested that doing so could potentially give me a working control of this company and that seemed like it might be a good idea. He hesitated and said he would get back to me. I'm still waiting! Instead, the shares of SGDE began to run up in price almost immediately.

I don't know for sure if my telephone call had anything to do with the run-up in price, but you can draw your own conclusions. Later that year I decided to meet the management of SGDE and made a trip to St. Paul to meet and speak to the management in person. After all, I owned a large number of shares that were now worth a good deal of money, and it is only logical for a large investor to want to look into the eyes of the people controlling the situation. Needless to say, I was impressed with them and their presentation. It was well worth the trip.

The share price of SGDE began to rise in a steady fashion from the time I established my position in the 2000–2001 time period at a slow consistent pace.

As it rose, several of my friends who had purchased some shares were more than happy to sell them at a nice profit at the $2 to $4 level. Who could blame them, considering how lousy the market was and virtually everything else they owned was in the "crapper"? However, I learned a long time ago that buy and sell decisions should be made based on where the stock is now rather than "where I bought it." The fact that one buys a stock at $1 doesn't mean it should be sold at $4 just because it is up. The proper way to make a decision on whether to buy or sell is to ask yourself, "If I didn't already own (or was short) these shares, would I buy or sell them now?" An honest, well-thought-out, unbiased answer to this question would usually help a person make the right decision. Usually, however, greed and fear overcome people's ability to think rationally, and in this situation, considering the times, they were more than happy to grab their profit and run. That decision was a big mistake.

Take Note

The proper way to make a decision on whether to buy or sell a stock is to ask yourself, "If I didn't already own (or was short) these shares, would I buy or sell them now?"

Concluding Thoughts

In 2002 the company began to perform incredibly well, fundamentally growing sales and earnings significantly in virtually every quarter up to the present. Its buyer's club has grown to several hundred thousand members, and in 2005 the company made a brilliant acquisition of the Golf Warehouse. The Golf Warehouse (TGW), the largest Internet seller of golf equipment in the country, was acquired for $30 million in cash and was accretive to earnings from the beginning. This was quite an accomplishment for a company that had a total market cap of less than $3 million a few years earlier.

Since 2002, the shares of SGDE have risen in virtually a continuously upward slope, to a split adjusted level of $46.50 a share, where it was taken over by a large foreign company. Many LPVSs go up several hundred or even thousands of percentage points, but very few go up like this one, which allowed an orderly exit point for all involved. SGDE is, and will always be, an LPVS classic.

8

Come and Get It:
Aptimus, Inc. (APTM)

Discovering an attractive low-priced value stock (LPVS) candidate, while not often difficult, can be a very challenging task. As discussed earlier, often one can find attractive candidates in their day-to-day activities by identifying interesting companies that provide goods and services familiar in their lifestyles (that new fast-food restaurant chain that you thought was great, that skin cream that worked miracles on your rash, that computer software that was immensely helpful, etc.). To identify a potentially lucrative LPVS, first one must know that they are structured as a corporation and that the corporation is publicly traded. Then one should determine through numerous available sources the market price, capitalization, and desirability of the company. If a company is in fact public, has acceptable fundamentals, and is trading at what appears to be an unrealistically low price, it may very well qualify as an LPVS candidate. The fact of the matter is that the vast majority of companies are not public and do not fit into the above criteria. Although good LPVS opportunities are out there, chances are, no one is going to point them out to you. One must make a conscious effort to be on the lookout for these opportunities regularly.

> ### Take Note
>
> To identify a potentially lucrative LPVS, first one must know that they are structured as a corporation and that the corporation is publicly traded. Then one should determine through numerous available sources the market price, capitalization, and desirability of the company.

From the Horse's Mouth

Despite the difficulty of identifying great candidates, sometimes these candidates are all but advertised to the public by the companies themselves. On occasion, companies that are selling at very attractive valuations try to take advantage of the extremely low market valuations by buying back their shares from ill-advised and complacent stockholders. Usually, this occurs during depressed market times at prices that often appear ludicrous (especially in hindsight). Companies and/or their management buying back their own shares are a prime source of attractive LPVS candidates. This information can be readily obtained through Securities and Exchange Commission (SEC) filings or several services that keep track of this corporate behavior. In general, if a company is willing to spend equity dollars, take dollars out of its treasury to buy back equity in times of depressed markets, it is usually a sure sign that the valuation of those shares is compelling. During market declines, and especially during market meltdowns, it is unusual for a company to commit its cash reserves on hand to the purchase of public equity because it may be very difficult for that company to replace this cash when needed. If the company decides to do this, it is usually proof positive that the shares are selling at "giveaway" prices. When cash is hard to come by, the last thing good management wants to do is reduce their cash reserves and potentially put themselves in a precarious position by using that cash to redeem a nonobligatory equity. In other words, common shares represent no obligation to the company; there is no compelling reason for them to buy back an ownership interest with dollars that could be used for more important obligations. The company has no obligation to buy common stock; they do have obligations to pay salaries, interest on their debt, accounts payable, rent, and a variety of other business expenses that require cash. During difficult times, the last thing most companies would choose to do is to reduce their cash reserves by buying back common shares of the company. Companies usually will do so only if they believe the common stock is absurdly cheap.

Take Note

During difficult times, the last thing most companies would choose to do is to reduce their cash reserves by buying back common shares of the company. Companies usually will do so only if they believe the common stock is absurdly cheap.

My conclusion is that if by following the local business news you find a company announcing the repurchase of a sizable amount of their own shares, it can very well mean that these shares are considered dramatically undervalued by the corporate management. Usually, if management is competent, they would be the most likely people to know what the value of the common stock is, because they are privy to more information about the company than anyone else, and it is a high probability that if they are buying it, it very well may be an attractive buy. Remember, however, there are reasons that companies buy back their own stock that don't have anything to do with dramatic undervaluation. Often, there are reasons having to do with options, compensation, sinking funds, and so on. By quickly perusing the buyback document, one can readily establish the reasons for the repurchase. A quick perusal of the financial statements will usually plainly reveal if a company is seriously undervalued when considering this security for LPVS status. The SEC regulations are fairly intense and usually require a company to state the reasons for the repurchase of the shares. If the shares are being repurchased for reasons other than low-valuation purposes, those reasons will typically be laid out in the tender document or corresponding news releases.

Aptimus Goes IPO

A classic example of a company that telegraphed to the world the significant undervaluation of its shares was Aptimus, Inc. (see Figure 8.1). Aptimus was taken public by a major Wall Street firm in early 2000 just before the Internet bubble burst. Aptimus's initial public offering (IPO) was priced at $18 per share by the underwriters (Aptimus's name was ultimately changed after originally coming out under the name FREESHOPS), and as was typical in early 2000, the stock, because of its Internet affiliation, opened for trading at around $60 per share. This was just days before the Internet bubble burst, and within a few months the shares of Aptimus declined to a price of twenty two...cents ($0.22). Not dollars—cents! Yes, the stock declined from over $60 a share to just a few pennies in just over one year's time—a time period so short that even the company itself was unable to lose all the money that it had raised in the IPO. Being astute businessmen, Aptimus's management soon realized that their shares were undervalued relative to their business prospects and were selling at such a small fraction of the cash they had on hand that they decided to take a portion of their remaining funds and buy back some shares from the public at a pittance of the current value of the shares and a tiny fraction of the original IPO price.

In the summer of 2001 Aptimus initiated a tender offer for $5 million worth of their company's common stock at a price of $0.48

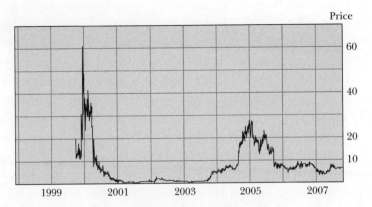

Figure 8.1   APTM: Aptimus, Inc., 1999–2007

Data source: Yahoo! Finance, Nasdaq.com

per share, an amount representing a significant premium to the then current price of just $0.22 and a substantial discount to the cash on hand and no consideration at all for any of the company's advancements and goodwill to date. The $5 million number was the amount of money needed to buy all the publicly traded shares out-standing—just over 10 million shares multiplied by the $0.48 price per share being offered to the public.

While in hindsight one might say that a price of $0.48 would be considered ludicrous for a company that had much more than that in cash alone, it still represented over a 100 percent increase in the current market price for the Aptimus shares at the time. Simply stated, the market price of Aptimus at the time the tender offer was made bore absolutely no relationship to the intrinsic value of the shares. Aptimus's shares were just being mindlessly liquidated by funds and individuals with no regard whatsoever to underlying value. The Internet bubble caused panic selling in virtually every se-curity that was in any way, shape, or form related to the Internet. The tender offer was made in August 2001 just a few short weeks before the 9/11 debacle. Before the 9/11 disaster, the overall market had already been very weak, especially in Internet stocks, and the new issue market had just about shut down. Small companies at this time were hard pressed to obtain additional financing for virtually any project, especially those that were Internet related. Despite these realities, Aptimus's management felt comfortable enough about their fundamental and financial situation to commit $5 million of its precious dollars plus expenses to the purchase of some of their publicly traded common stock. Once again, common stock is not a financial liability to a company and is usually the last type of security that a company would commit scarce cash to acquire.

Take Note

Common stock is not a financial liability to a company and is usually the last type of security that a company would commit scarce cash to before paying more pressing matters like salaries, interest on their debt, accounts payable, and rent, to name just a few. If you see a com-pany buying them, it's a strong affirmation of the value of the shares.

What did the scenario described say to an experienced LPVS investor? It said that the people who were the most informed about this company were willing to buy its shares at well above the current market price, using very sacred cash reserves that could not readily be replaced in the foreseeable future—a very, very strong affirmation of the value of the shares. The tender documents specifically stated that the management was not advising people to sell these shares, but rather was only giving them an opportunity to receive a significant premium from the current market price and, more importantly, providing significant liquidity for those stockholders who felt compelled to liquidate their shares in this tumultuous market decline and Internet panic. Even when the company had the opportunity to cancel their offer after the tragic 9/11 event (utilizing a marketout clause), they chose to continue the offer and extend it awhile longer. This was an absolute affirmation of their confidence in their decision to retire the company's shares.

To a logically thinking LPVS investor, Aptimus was screaming to the investment world that they believed their shares were grossly undervalued and were willing to put their money where their mouth was. To my mind, these types of actions are certainly convincing enough to commit some of my capital to these shares. Even though the tender documents continuously advised the investors that management was not recommending the sale of these securities, the overwhelming sentiment in the economy was extremely negative, and market circumstances convinced most owners of the shares to ignore this boilerplate advice.

The Ins and Outs of Electronic Communications Networks (ECNs)

I began acquiring the shares of Aptimus strictly as a trading vehicle to scalp and earn ECN fees. The fundamentals of the company was something I glanced at just to give myself peace of mind that the company would not likely go out of business while I was doing my trading. I usually trade these low-priced stocks from the long side because they cannot go down to less than zero: a price that usually isn't that far away. Shorting a low-priced stock has very minimal profit potential because a stock can't go below zero, and therefore short profits in low-priced stocks are seldom worth the inherent risk.

For those of you who aren't up to date on ECNs and rebate trading, simply stated, several brokerage firms allow people to receive a percentage of the ECN fees generated when one bids or offers for a stock on an ECN. When the contrary side "hits the bid" or "takes the offer," an ECN fee is generated. While these fees are usually only a small fraction of a cent, when multiplied by a large number of shares, they can very often represent a significant profit for the client even on a trade where no price differential is earned. The fees alone can often create sizable percentage gains for the client. Therefore, by trading many thousands of shares of a low-priced stock such as Aptimus, significant percentage returns could be earned simply by earning the ECN fee rebates given by the dealer. The fact that Aptimus was trading at such a low price enabled large quantities of shares to be moved back and forth without committing a sizable amount of capital to the position.

Due to this, when Aptimus announced the tender offer in August 2001, I was fortunate enough to immediately have a good profit on the long shares I was carrying, and this gave me the opportunity to look closer at the fundamentals of the situation. In general, I had no desire fundamentally to be invested in Internet stocks at this point in time. Nevertheless, the fundamental opportunity being shouted by management in the tender documents did not fall on deaf ears. I realized very quickly that the number of shares that they were tendering for was essentially the entire float outstanding and that the $0.48 price put a bottom on the shares. The management indicated that they would not be selling any of their "inside holdings," and therefore the company would be obliged to accept every share tendered. At this point, it was obvious to me that even if I bought the stock up to $0.48 per share and earned only an ECN rebate fee for buying it on the bid, a significant riskless rate of return would be available.

As a trader, I learned early on that if one could have potentially excellent upside gain and virtually no downside exposure, this was good. Also, I learned early on that even when things look virtually riskless, "things happen" that can screw up even what seems to be a sure thing. In the case of Aptimus, the "thing" that very well might have screwed up my virtually riskless arbitrage was 9/11, an event so horrendous it needs no further explanation. Aptimus's management could have readily used a "market-out" clause to suspend or cancel its tender due to the market conditions. If that had occurred, the shares of Aptimus would have probably gone down to where they had traded prior to the tender and perhaps even substantially lower, resulting in a significant percentage loss in the shares. This sort of percentage decline would have been more painful than I care to think about. Fortunately for me, and once again confirming in my mind the value of these shares, management decided to damn the torpedoes and went full speed ahead, extending the offer despite the tragedy, and remained firm in their commitment to buy back shares despite the craziness of this time. At this point, I wanted to buy these shares more than ever and continued to bid aggressively for the shares.

The final extension for the tender offer ended in early November 2001, at which point all shares that could or would be tendered had to have been sent to the company for acceptance. A couple of days before the expiration I had to decide how many shares of my holdings I wanted to tender. My holdings now totaled several hundred thousand shares, an amount certainly greater than I wanted to hold even though I loved the situation.

Tendering Shares

After a period of extensive deliberation, I decided to tender the majority of my shares and to hold back approximately 200,000 shares as a kicker. My belief was that, since the stock was strongly bid at $0.48 a share in the open market for a period of several weeks, most of the shares would have been tendered. As a matter of fact, for a short period of time, I bid $0.49 a share in an effort to test the market to see if a sizable number of shares would come in for sale at a price above the tender price. Logically speaking, if one were contemplating tendering their shares at $0.48 a share, they would certainly be motivated to take an even higher price in the open market. The fact of the matter was that very few shares were sold to me even at a price that exceeded the tender price. My conclusion was that very few of the 10.3 million shares of the public float would be tendered. My educated guess was that the company would receive somewhere between 1 and 2 million shares at best, and that included the several hundred thousand shares that I planned to tender.

To my surprise, the company received approximately 9.4 million shares in response to the tender, an amount so large that to this day it is still one of the most illogical events I have ever experienced on Wall Street. The irrational behavior of the investment community relative to this stock and the times in general has indelibly made an impression on my mind. What this told me was that the investment community is not efficient and herd mentality overwhelms logic all too often. To think that over 90 percent of the public holders of Aptimus would give away their shares at a price not even close to a price resembling fair value was shocking and almost scary. (Simply stated, the results of this tender, in my mind, bordered on investment insanity.) After the results of the tender were disseminated, the market-making community, in all of its wisdom, chose to quote the stock at an initially lower price.

As I told you, I find market makers, in general, among the least sophisticated people on Wall Street. Perhaps it is not their fault. Market makers seldom analyze or have any substantive thoughts about the value of the stocks they trade. In most cases, the share prices are just numbers, and other than using those numbers to scalp a few pennies, nothing else really matters. Taking the shares down must have seemed logical, considering the fact that the buyers had completed their buying and naturally no one else in the world would want to own these shares. The fact that less than 1 million shares remained in the float, of which I held 20 percent, made little difference in their quoting of the market. Remember, the shares that were tendered and accepted by the company would never be available for resale again. They were taken into the treasury and were no longer available for resale. The entire float now had a total market value of a mere few hundred thousand dollars, yet the company had millions of dollars left in cash.

Take Note

Market makers seldom analyze the value of the stocks they trade. In most cases, the share prices are just numbers they use to scalp a few pennies here or there.

Realizing the brilliance of their move to quote the stock lower, I once again began to buy shares from these geniuses who were selling them. I bought several thousand more shares slightly below to slightly above the tender price. After buying several thousand shares more over the next few weeks, I believe that some of these dealers who were selling the shares short may have had an epiphany, might have looked a little more closely at what they were selling and said to themselves, "oops." The stock soon traded up to the $1.25 to $1.50 level. I believe a short squeeze was in process because this almost 200 percent increase in price was against a backdrop of a still very negative stock market. I maintained a bid for these shares on a regular basis, utilizing ECNs. I knew the short situation was prevalent because one day when I went out for lunch my bid for a few hundred shares was filled on the ECN and within a matter of minutes, on virtually no volume, the market makers, who were most likely short the stock, downticked the quotation from a $1.25 bid down to a $0.25 bid (almost $1 a share, which was almost 80 percent of its value) with no news, no explanation, no justification. I didn't know whether to laugh or cry when I got back from lunch, but the signal they gave me was clear: the market makers were "short and caught" and "hurtin' for certain." I used this opportunity to buy some more shares back at the ludicrously low valuation, but within a very short period of time the stock was back at the $1.50 level.

Concluding Thoughts

Over the next few months, the stock pretty much languished around the $1 level, not because the stock was overpriced or underpriced, but because no one gave a damn about LPVSs at this time. Then the company started to talk about some of their successes, retained a public relations firm, and raised some fresh capital, and suddenly the shares began an extraordinary rise in price, which few stocks ever experience. Over the next year, the shares moved up from under $1 to in excess of $27 a share.

All the while the stock traded with good volume and ready liquidity. This run-up of several thousand percentage points, while very impressive, was not totally a big surprise. Remember, this stock did come out at $18 a share as an IPO and traded to in excess of

$60 a share in the aftermarket. The major underwriter that took the company public did believe the company had a substantial future. This extraordinary rise could not be called totally unexpected or dumb luck. The profit potential that was realized was more because of the unrealistic undervaluation that was created by an irrational market than it was by dumb luck, promotion, or an unexpected market occurrence.

If you look at the facts, what happened here was not totally unexpected, unlike a major medical breakthrough or a big oil discovery or some other unexpected development that creates a major rise in its stock price. These shares rose primarily because they were far too undervalued to begin with, and most of the rise was just a reevaluation of a completely distorted view that happened during the Internet bubble and debacle. The value was there and the price was low, which equals an LPVS.

Take Note

When the value is there and the price is low, that is a good LPVS situation.

CHAPTER 9

Forgotten Stocks that Fill a Niche: Aduddell Industries (ADDL)

The interesting thing about some low-priced forgotten stocks is their ability to sometimes rise from the dead. Occasionally, a company that for all practical purposes is a failure, meaning it has become insolvent, bankrupt, or otherwise inactive for a variety of reasons, can get a new lease on life. This reality is due to the fact that as a former public company, the "public" nature of the entity gives it value because it can potentially be resurrected as a public shell. Many formerly failed public entities have come back to life and relative success (stock value–wise) because the public shell was reorganized by any number of corporate maneuvers.

Public Shells

A good, clean public shell can be worth upwards of a half million dollars to investors or other corporate entities that desire to become a publicly traded corporate entity without the hassle, time, and expense of going through a formal public offering. Very often, the marketplace is not strong enough for brokerage firms to place new issues for any number of reasons and the new public offering route is not even an option. For example, the market for new issues has been almost nonexistent since the Internet meltdown of 2000. In the past six years only a relatively few companies have gone public via the new-issue route, and usually those that did were the higher-quality private companies with good credentials. The availability of new issue money for the more speculative venture-type deals has dried up significantly since the Internet debacle of 2000 when Wall Street was throwing money at any piece of crap that had "Internet" in its name. Naturally, the insanity that gave rise to the Internet debacle has now created the difficult environment for new-issue financing for all new deals. The unrestrained greed of Wall Street's bagging the investment community with billions of dollars' worth of pure Internet "crap" had come home to roost.

There are a variety of reasons why a company would want to be public even if it didn't raise new money in a public offering. The main benefit of being public is that it allows a corporate entity to create a new form of currency, which can be used for any number of corporate objectives. Very often, "restricted" shares can be issued by a public entity to help in the compensating of a variety of employees, consultants, directors, advisers, lawyers, accountants, and so on. Many people are more than willing to take stock in lieu of monetary compensation if they believe the new entity has the potential of being a big success. They are especially happy to take stock in a newly reorganized public shell if it is being publicly quoted and traded and therefore has at least a "perceived" real value. The reality is that very often the quoted market is not very "deep," meaning there are only a small number of shares trading at the quoted prices; nevertheless, people often prefer to see a real number attached to the shares they receive. This new currency can also be issued by the newly reorganized public shell company to acquire other businesses or assets for "stock" or any other form of corporate securities based on a publicly traded vehicle (e.g., convertible bonds, preferred stock, warrants, rights). Naturally, this currency can be quite an effective tool in the hands of competent businessmen who can use it for corporate good. Unfortunately, there are many promoters who are all too willing to hype up a public shell and once again use their promotional talents to fleece public investors. That is why I spent so much time earlier differentiating between penny stocks and low-priced value stocks (LPVSs).

Take Note

Many people are more than willing to take stock in lieu of monetary compensation if they believe the new entity has the potential of being a big success.

However, there are several negatives to going public through the public shell route. The primary reason is the expense of acquiring the shell and the fact that there is no new equity money coming in from the public offering. In addition, there are other continuing expenses in maintaining the public status: regulatory filings, accounting obligations and shareholders' surveillance of all your activities. You now have potentially thousands of partners, and all too often they always have something to say. Unless the benefits of being public significantly outweigh the advantages of staying private, it is very questionable if going public through a public shell is advisable.

If a public shell is restructured properly by people who are truly looking to build value and not necessarily looking to screw the original public shareholders who owned the pre-restructured shares, the potential for extraordinary profits may be at hand. One such example of this is Zenex Corporation (now Aduddell Industries, Inc.), a company that failed in its original business dealings but was restructured through an acquisition into a corporate shell and went on to subsequently have its reorganized shares go up in price by almost 2,000 percent.

Take Note

If a public shell is restructured properly, the potential for extraordinary profits may be at hand.

Acquiring Aduddell

Aduddell Industries (ADDL), Inc. (see Figure 9.1), through its subsidiaries, currently operates in the commercial roofing industry

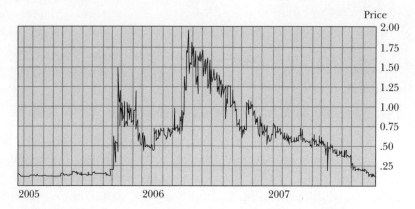

Figure 9.1 Aduddell Industries, Inc. (ADDL), 2005–2007

Data source: Yahoo! Finance, Nasdaq.com

in the United States. It offers various roofing services, including reroofing, maintenance, restoration and repair, resurfacing, new roof construction, sheet metal fabrication, and waterproofing to corporate clients and governmental agencies. It offers these services to industrial, office, retail, hospitality, government, and educational industries. ADDL was formerly known as Lone Wolf Energy, Inc., which was founded in 1976. It changed its name to Zenex Telecom, Inc. in 2001; to Zenex International, Inc., in 2002; and to Aduddell Industries, Inc., in June 2006. Aduddell Industries is based in Oklahoma City, Oklahoma.

After the new roofing business was merged into Zenex, the stock traded for months at between the $0.10 and $0.15 level. Millions of shares changed hands at this level, making it entirely possible for an interested party to acquire literally millions of shares of stock if one so desired. In this particular situation, no special trading techniques needed to be employed in order to accumulate a significant position, just a steady bid present in the market. This could be accomplished with a limit order placed with a market maker or, better yet, the use of an electronic communications network (ECN) qualified to represent orders on bulletin board stocks. Not all ECNs offer the ability to place orders on bulletin board stocks, but a few do, including ARCA, TRAC, and EDGX. Why all ECNs don't offer this service is a mystery to me, but I'm sure they have their reasons. Maintaining a minimally higher bid on these shares than the other bidders and market makers would have all but assured success in the acquisition of the number of shares desired.

I began acquiring these shares at the suggestion of my brother-in-law, who brought this situation to my attention. As an over-the-counter (OTC) trader in my employ, he often mentioned stocks he felt looked like potential value plays. Joel, who has been a penny-stock specialist almost his entire career, spanning over 40 years, usually didn't differentiate between penny stocks and LPVSs, but rather traded them as numbers. Several years ago as we were working and sitting next to each other, I finally convinced him that accumulating and placing LPVSs was a far better idea than getting involved with the usual garbage being touted in the penny-stock world. Naturally, as a dealer in low-priced stocks of all kinds, most of the trading activity was in the "crap" penny stocks, and therefore much of a market maker's trading profits were made in those stocks. The LPVSs typically trade far less often, and the big profits in LPVSs come by holding positions—not an option most market makers are afforded by their firms. Joel is now a staunch supporter of my LPVS theories and occasionally shows me situations that he believes are good, overlooked value plays.

Dealers and traders almost never commit capital or invest in the stocks they trade, and that is a primary reason why very often there are such major fluctuations in prices, even if a relatively small number of shares actually change hands in a particular security. Market makers and specialists who are supposedly charged with maintaining orderly markets are usually a primary cause of major swings in intraday market price fluctuations. Unless dealers have customer buy or sell orders in a particular stock at specified price levels, they will very seldom step up to the plate and stabilize the market in those shares by using their own capital. On the contrary, they will often exasperate the move by aggressively moving the quote in the direction of least resistance. That is why if you have an interest in accumulating any meaningful amount of an LPVS, it is incumbent upon you to place your orders strategically in the marketplace to assure execution; if not, they will be traded through and around, neither of which does you any good.

Take Note

Market makers and specialists who are supposedly charged with maintaining orderly markets are usually a primary cause of major swings in intraday market price fluctuations.

Remember, dealers, market makers, specialists, and other various Wall Street middlemen are not your friends. As I've said before, they are money-grubbers attempting to make your money theirs—as much as they can get away with, without getting caught. If you think the regulators (Securities and Exchange Commission [SEC], National Association of Securities Dealers [NASD], New York Stock Exchange [NYSE], etc.) will prevent or stop Wall Street's abuse, you're kidding yourself. Many of the regulators worked for the industry in the past or are attempting to work for them in the future; forget about justice or fair and timely adjudication.

You must do everything in your power to prevent being abused and taken advantage of. Use limit orders and demand that your orders be displayed properly. Use computerized order entry programs to assure that there is no confusion as to the order that is being placed: name of stock, number of shares, buy or sell, price, exact time of order entry, and so on. Keep abreast of the price fluctuations in the stock and don't be afraid to demand a report (fill) if you see the stock trade at your limit level, and especially if you see the market trade through your limit. Don't let yourself be abused by brokerages that are more concerned with making their industry friends happy and richer with your hard-earned money.

Finding Zenex (ZENX)

I started buying the ZENX shares at about $0.12. The company at the time was earning a small amount of money and was selling at a very low price-earnings (P/E) multiple. This business was relatively mundane, but it seemed to fill a very real need. It was a forgotten stock with virtually no following or sponsorship in the investment community, and although it had over 40 million shares outstanding, its market capitalization was still exceptionally low, and therefore this situation met most of my LPVS criteria. Buying ZENX was no problem, and it was only a matter of how large a position I wanted to accumulate. When I say it was no problem I mean that if I were willing to pay up an additional penny, many tens of thousands of shares were readily available, although at $0.12 a share an additional penny is about a 12½ percent increase in price. This percentage increase is relevant only in neutral times because if I had known then that in a matter of months this stock would be trading at almost $2 a share, an additional penny would hardly have been relevant. When investing in LPVSs, a penny or two increment should, in most cases, be considered irrelevant because if you turn out to be wrong, what's the difference if you paid $0.12 or $0.13 a share? If the stock is going to zero, whether you paid a penny more or less makes little difference in the total amount lost. However, if a $0.12 stock winds up going to $2 a share and you did not buy it because you were trying to save a penny by bidding for the shares rather than taking the offer, that would be the height of stupidity and aggravation.

The major consideration when investing in an LPVS like ZENX is how much money on a dollar basis should be committed to the situation? Remember, when first getting involved with a new LPVS, you don't know for sure whether it will explode to the upside, languish, or fall into oblivion. Naturally, if your analysis is right more often than wrong, the percentages are certainly in your favor. A winner in the LPVS arena can easily return several hundred percentage points of profit, while an absolute loser will cost you a maximum of 100 percent of the dollar amount of the money you invested. Keeping the dollar amounts invested in numerous LPVSs balanced should be attempted so that you do not expose yourself to disproportionate losses if some of your choices go awry.

Despite the best analysis and judicious use of common sense, it never hurts to have a little good luck on your side. Yes, ZENX had a good little roofing business, made some money, had competent management, had a reasonable capitalization, and was trading at a low P/E, but the one thing that made this stock explode had nothing to do with any of that. The home-run factor for ZENX was a horrible hurricane season in 2004 and 2005. Rita, Katrina, and Wilma were the ladies that were charmed for ZENX. These horrendous storms caused such damage to the southeastern United States that ZENX received so much roofing work as to create a dream situation for anyone in the roofing industry. Factor in a few tornadoes, twisters, tropical storms, and other various quirks of nature and you have an investment opportunity seldom based on such strong business fundamentals. Barring massive incompetence, this company should have a virtually limitless backlog of profitable work for the foreseeable future.

Take Note

A winner in the LPVS arena can easily return several hundred percentage points of profit, while an absolute loser will cost you a maximum of 100 percent of the dollar amount of the money you invested. Keeping the dollar amounts invested in numerous LPVSs balanced should be your goal so that you do not expose yourself to disproportionate losses if some of your choices go awry.

With the above as a backdrop, ZENX (now Aduddell Industries, remember) rose steadily to just a hair shy of $2 a share. Based on my original investment, this represented approximately a 1,500 percent rise in price. Naturally, I sold a portion of my position as it rose, but I did scale out my shares in an orderly fashion and retained some of my stock into the highest levels. Once again, I continually asked myself that famous question, "If I didn't already own these shares, would I want to own them here?" That question's answer was usually "yes," and that is why I retained shares throughout the run-up. I did sell some at various levels because another well-known saying is, "You'll never go broke taking some profits," and, I'll be honest, the temptation to cash in is always a strong one, especially when there are usually many downward gyrations during the trading day.

Concluding Thoughts

ADDL traded for several months after I liquidated my position at approximately $1.50 a share. However, I believed it, at that level, to be only fairly undervalued and not necessarily cheap. Since I believe in finding significantly undervalued and/or grossly ignored stocks, ZENX/ADDL no longer held its former attraction in my eyes. That doesn't mean I won't trade it from time to time if I see a good entry point, but I will probably not hold a meaningful investment position at a neutral price level. If it drops down closer to its former level, I will most assuredly reassess my opinion and take appropriate action.

10

A Lesson in Management: Gencor Industries, Inc. (GENC)

As discussed in the previous chapter, the actions of management often can be the treasure map in finding truly undervalued low-priced stocks. First, let's understand a reality of investing: when you buy a stock, it is being sold to you by a contrary party who, for all practical purposes, believes that the shares he owns are probably fully or at least fairly priced, and that is why he is selling them. As I've said before, because it's such an important point, a trade by definition is a difference in opinion—the person buying a stock believes it is probably undervalued and will probably rise in price for whatever reason she believes to be valid; conversely, the seller of the shares most likely believes the shares are at a level that is high enough for him to swap cash for the shares he owns. While this is a simplistic approach to buying and selling, in the greater scheme of things it is really simply the basis of the market. What information is available to whom is probably the greatest factor in determining which side of a transaction will be more or less aggressive. For years, the regulatory authorities have looked to make the playing field fairer by passing rules and regulations that try to make the dissemination of pertinent information fair and equitable for all parties. And if you believe that, I have a bridge to sell you. But I digress....

Information is rarely disseminated fairly and equally to the investment public. Various entities, sometimes called insiders, are often privileged to information not readily available to the average investor—that's why many people who are active in the market believe that the actual trading in shares of many companies really tells you more about what might be going on than the numerous news releases and financial information disseminated by the company and other knowledgeable sources. When stocks that apparently have had no current or recent information being disseminated are inexplicably rising or falling in price, there is a good chance that something is transpiring, despite the apparent lack of any news. Astute traders often watch this type of activity in a stock for telltale events, which may indicate that something is going on beyond the scope of the publicly disseminated information.

Many low-priced value stocks (LPVSs) are trading at an extremely low price for a myriad of reasons. These reasons are often orchestrated by the companies themselves for unholy agendas, which often benefit the management or current insiders. If, in fact, a company that, for all practical purposes, logically should be trading at a higher price due to overwhelming fundamental reasons is not doing so, take notice.

Take Note

If a company that, for all practical purposes, logically should be trading at a higher price due to overwhelming fundamental reasons is not doing so, take notice.

Management Maneuvering

When a company's shares are trading at an evaluation that seems ludicrously low, often management and the insiders see this low valuation as a slap in their face from the public market and may in fact grow to resent the market for ignoring their efforts and their supposed successes. Being ignored and overlooked is often a psychological situation that creates inappropriate responses from the persons or entity being shunned. In the case of public companies, often a management team, rather than continuing what appears to be its futile effort to enhance the valuation of its shares, makes a decision to do just the opposite. The management actually helps to depress the shares as much as they can by any means they believe they can get away with. Then, at some point, they look to "hoodwink" the public by buying back from the public, at this self-achieved severely reduced price, the shares they helped and contrived to create.

Management, rather than trying to enhance share value, may be so frustrated and resentful that they may, in fact, begin to subconsciously resent the shareholders and the market in general and start thinking of ways to do just the opposite of what their mandate or charge is: to enhance stockholders' value. I have seen this phenomenon all too often in the LPVS sector as shares of the forgotten companies tend to languish in the state of oblivion for months and even years at a time. Then management will do whatever is in their power to depress further the already ignored and depressed shares by using devious techniques, which has the effect of making a bad situation look even worse than it may really be.

When the shares of the company then continue to fall to inconsequential valuations, this same management may look to take the company private or issue large numbers of new shares based on this absurdly low valuation. This enables the unprincipled management to literally steal the company from the very shareholders who have chosen to stick with the situation and maintain a confidence in the management's potential ability to enhance the value of their shares. Unfortunately, this scenario occurs all too often on Wall Street, and little is done by our supposed regulators to prevent such abuses from being perpetrated.

Because these companies are often small and thinly traded, the staff at the regulator's office often choose to ignore these situations because of their lack of mass public interest. No kudos or feathers in their hat will be realized by punishing this type of offender due to the limited number of stockholders that may still hold the shares of these small companies. Regulators are often regulators strictly because of their desire to gain experience and go on to work in the private sector. In the private sector they can earn far greater salaries and attain far greater recognition than working as a federal or state regulator. Therefore, spending much time on what they believe to be relatively small and inconsequential violations is usually not in their personal best interest, and as a result, numerous atrocities can occur in situations involving these small, publicly traded companies strictly because nobody cares. Even the business press seems to pay little attention to these types of abuses for the same basic reasoning. Because the market cap of the affected LPVSs is usually small in total dollar terms, seldom is there a stockholder with a large enough vested interest in these shares willing to spend the amount of money needed to litigate against these shady management groups. They usually will systematically use the company's own money (your money) to defend their immoral/illegal activities. Even the supposed laws that have been passed to protect shareholders against corrupt management, such as the Sarbanes-Oxley Act, are really toothless farces that have very limited and unobtainable remedies for the average investors in small companies. These laws were written to be deliberately toothless and have little, if any, use if you are not a governmental agency.

The extent to which a devious management/inside group would go to intentionally depress the value of their shares is almost limitless. Greed is a very intense emotion, and this emotion can cause people who would normally be honest and forthright to start looking for excuses to become deceptive and manipulating.

Maneuvering for Opportunity

While this scenario might scare away most investors from participating in an investment in such a company, this type of situation can often prove itself to be an extraordinary investment opportunity for a determined LPVS investor who is not afraid to rattle the cage of a company that is participating in this type of unseemly behavior. The most important factor an LPVS investor must possess is the fact that he is right in conjunction with the questionable behavior of the management. If the LPVS investor is willing to shed light on the factors he believes are pertinent, the ploy being perpetrated by the target company can often be derailed, and, hopefully, the value of the severely depressed shares can once again start to reflect the intrinsic value.

Take Note

LPVS investors must truly believe that they are correct in their analysis of the management's behavior, devious or principled.

Perhaps my best example of this scenario is a company in which I have owned a very sizable position for many years, Gencor Industries, Inc. (symbol: GENC). Gencor Industries (see Figure 10.1), a company involved for years in producing equipment for the road construction and asphalt industry, traded at various levels and had varying degrees of success and failures all through the 1980s and 1990s. They experienced significant difficulties and various amounts of success during this period, but going into the late 1990s they seemed to have put their act together and became a substantive company with significant sales and earnings with a stock that traded to approximately $29 a share on the American Exchange (AMEX). The management always believed their shares were significantly undervalued, demonstrated by the fact that they seldom, if ever, sold any of

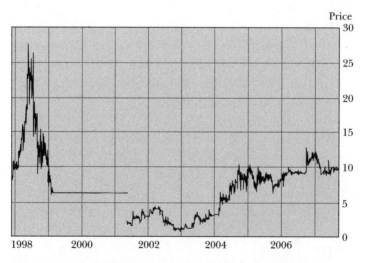

Figure 10.1   Gencor Industries Inc. (GENC), 1998–2008

Data source: Yahoo! Finance, Nasdaq.com

their shares into the market even at the highest levels established in 1998. Their success was in great part due to the management's ability to acquire and assimilate several related companies into the parent company and make them accretive to earnings almost immediately. Even when the stock was trading near its all-time highs, management believed their shares to be dramatically undervalued and seldom issued new shares for acquisition, but rather used cash and debt to finance their takeovers.

In late 1998, when the company seemed to be firing on all cylinders, they encountered a problem with a small British subsidiary, which they had acquired a short time earlier. Apparently, there had been some fraud and malfeasance in the accounting at the acquired company, which set off a chain of events that proved to be apparently devastating to Gencor and to its stockholders. The reason I say "apparently" is that I will always question the subsequent chain of events that occurred. Were they the way things had to be, or were there in fact diabolical schemes developed to depress the shares of the company for unholy and selfish reasons?

After the British accounting problems came to the surface, the company claimed to have to restated their earnings due to the problem. What seemed to be a minor problem relative to the overall size of Gencor caused a precipitous drop in the price of their shares from the high $20s to just over $6 a share, just before the AMEX halted trading in the shares. The specific details of what was going on at that time are hard to know for sure because the company was far from being forthright in releasing details of the problem, only alleging major problems with their accountants and auditors. To make matters worse, the company unilaterally decided to initiate a news blackout on what was going on and ceased filing any Securities and Exchange Commission (SEC) disclosure documents during the period of early 1999 through the end of 2001. I don't believe they had any legal or justifiable right to unilaterally discharge themselves of these disclosure duties, but they did so regardless. For over one year from the AMEX trading halt, Gencor did not trade at all until the end of June 2000, when it once began to trade in the pink sheets at prices well below $1 per share and momentarily even as low as $0.25. During this period the company chose to enter into chapter 11 bankruptcy protection for no real, apparent purpose. Apparently, the creditors were demanding repayment of their loans, and the obvious distaste that they had for management caused them to take a very aggressive stance, even though the company was still making a sizable amount of money from their operations, which never had really ceased. Court records showed that the bankruptcy judge himself could not understand why the company was in his courtroom filing for chapter 11 since they were making millions of dollars.

By the end of 2001, the dust settled and all creditors were paid off in full (including interest); the company came out of chapter 11 in a very strong position except for the fact that the stockholders basically had their clocks cleaned. The stock, which had been trading in the high $20s before these events, was now trading in the $1 to $2 range. One might be inclined to suspect that much of the trauma that took place during this period was in fact orchestrated, in an attempt by the management and insiders to take full possession of this once fine public company. I say this because, shortly after coming out of bankruptcy, the company began to earn sizable amounts of money from an investment they had made prior to these problems in late 1998.

Apparently, in 1997, Gencor was contracted to build four synthetic coal production plants for a large financial consortium that planned to take advantage of the Clinton tax credit programs being offered to synthetic fuel operations. The program granted very generous tax credits for the production of enhanced synthetic coal. The problem that existed at the time was that this financial consortium had not yet completed raising the money for the production of these plants, which were required to be in operation and production of the synthetic fuel by no later than the end of June 1998. To help the situation, Gencor agreed to build these plants without advance payment to enable them to be ready on a timely basis. For this, Gencor was given a 20 percent interest in the general partner's interest in the project. Payment in full was to be made by the consortium, which included major utility firms and other financial interests, by March 1, 1998. When that date came, the money was still not available, and the consortium agreed to increase Gencor's interest by 5 percent for a 30-day extension. Subsequently, there were delays; extension after extension was granted by Gencor to the consortium/Carbontronics until the final closing, at the end of June 1998, when Gencor ended up with a total of a 45 percent interest in this project. These facts had to be obtained from court documents and other sources because the company never readily disclosed any of this to its public stockholders.

Since that time the company has earned tens of millions of dollars on this business interest and has virtually never fully disseminated all the relevant information about this holding to its stockholders. Gencor has had single quarters in which it has earned over $10 million from this investment (over $1 a share), yet little disclosure or substantive information has yet to come forth. When queried about this topic at an annual meeting, all the president of the company would say is that this incredible amount of income is like "manna from heaven." Despite this incredibly large amount of manna (money) being earned and the overall desirability of their being in the infrastructure and synthetic fuel business, the management allowed the company's shares to languish in the Pink Sheets and subsequently on the Bulletin Board. Virtually little to no effort was made by management to make the public aware of their successes. This "manna" has created a super-undervalued LPVS that only had to overcome an unconcerned management.

Recently, what the company calls its core business—its asphalt and road construction operations—has been doing exceptionally well. Its closest competitors' stocks (TEX, ASTE, etc.) have reached major all-time highs by rising hundreds of percentage points in price over the last few years, while Gencor's shares have languished. By any reasonable valuation and/or analysis, Gencor is trading at a ludicrous level, primarily due to management's former "screw the stockholders" attitude. After 30 years of being involved in this situation, it has always been my opinion that this too would pass as new proxy regulations from the SEC become law, and simply because the company's outstanding fundamentals would overwhelm even this management malaise. Hopefully, they will see the light and do the right thing to maximize shareholder value.

To this end, in late 2007, the company seems to have had an epiphany and has begun to do virtually everything right. Included among the positive actions are the relisting of their shares on the Nasdaq market, building the largest backlog of infrastructure equipment orders in their history, accumulating almost a hundred million dollars in cash and marketable securities, having no debt, and beginning a needed expansion of their production facilities and staff to meet an ever-increasing demand. They retained a competent investment banker (Morgan Keegan & Co., Inc.) to explore strategic alliances and combinations in an major move to grow and expand. Most importantly in my mind is their apparent attitude change as to maximizing shareholder value. This combination should prove to be just what the doctor ordered and I expect very gratifying results.

Concluding Thoughts

Gencor was a classic LPVS that has evolved into a super-cheap value stock. At current price levels, many people wouldn't call it a typical LPVS on a price basis, for purposes of this text, but by more traditional institutional or conventional standards, this stock must be considered as cheap as they come. Gencor is an instance of a winner LPVS, going from low-priced (penny-stock-like) status, to a higher-priced value stock category, but still being so undervalued as to give it the upside potential of an undiscovered LPVS, Price level alone is but one determinant of value. It just seems that on a percentage basis comparison, my experience shows that the greatest percentage returns are often achieved on lower-priced stocks, all things being equal, but tremendous returns can also be attained in higher-priced value if they too have been ignored or overlooked. As discussed earlier, the fact is that most of the more sizable investors will only invest in higher-priced securities and often shy away from the lower-priced issues.

Take Note

Price level alone is but one determinant of value.

11

More Illuminating LPVS Situations

A Company Regroups: Opko Health
(Formerly eXegenics [EXEG])

Opko Health, Inc., formerly eXegenics, Inc. and Cytoclonal Pharmaceuticals (see Figure 11.1), was historically engaged in the discovery and development of drugs for the treatment of cancers and drug-resistant bacterial diseases. In the past, they attempted to employ their various proprietary technologies to create low-molecular-weight "core inhibitor" molecules of disease-causing enzymes and proteins, which they hoped would accelerate and enhance the discovery and creation of novel drugs. Unfortunately, even the best-laid plans of even the smartest people do not always come to fruition, and eXegenic's research-and-development (R&D) efforts did not produce the successes they had hoped for.

A New Direction

In 2003, the board of directors apparently felt that the future prospects for the R&D work they had performed up to that time did not have the commercial potential they had originally hoped for. Rather than dissipate the remaining several million dollars they had left, they wisely just suspended operations, cut expenses to the maximum, and began to explore the various alternatives a company with significant cash and a publicly traded vehicle could capitalize on.

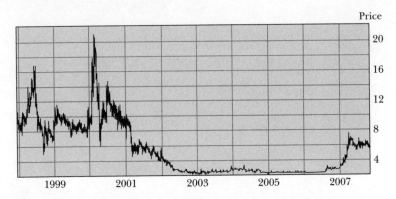

Figure 11.1 OPK: Opko Health, Inc. (formerly eXegenics, Inc.), 1998–2008

Data source: Yahoo! Finance, Nasdaq.com

The stock languished for the next few years and eventually traded down to about 50 percent of their underlying cash per share, which was approximately $0.30. The management did an admirable job by not slowly squandering their cash hoard and through prudent business activities explored many alternatives. Further, they came up with a business plan combining a number of new ideas, including developing a relationship with a new management affiliation, Dr. Philip Frost, formerly chairman of Ivax and Key Pharmaceuticals, who, with a net worth of approximately $1.2 billion, has been on the Forbes 400 list of America's wealthiest people.

In the first quarter of 2007, the company's stock traded up over 1,000 percent because of the excitement and renewed optimism that was created by EXEGs new business arrangement. The fact that the company had a sizable amount of cash and a clean shell remaining allowed the stock to trade so high.

eXegenics traded to almost $15 a share in the late 1990s, then got slammed down to a tiny fraction ($0.29). Because it was a low-priced value stock (LPVS) when it was trading at a fraction of its cash, the potential of a rebirth was well in place, and a huge profit potential existed. A primary reason the management of this company chose to cut expenses to the bare bones and not squander the cash on hand was that the managers did in fact hold a sizable position, which made their profit potential far greater than systematically siphoning off the company's remaining cash. Based on the stock's trading in excess of a 1,000 percent premium to where it was just one year earlier, it seems they made a "good" decision. I am pleased to say that I enjoyed a good ride on these shares, as well, although not nearly as much as some other situations I've traded.

As the eXegenics deal depicts, in general, buying low-priced stocks at a fraction of cash and marketable securities on hand is usually a good bet. As mentioned in earlier chapters, however, there are always exceptions to this scenario. Even so, cash-rich, debt-free companies are great prospects in your hunt for the perfect LPVS.

Take Note

Cash-rich, debt-free companies are great prospects in your hunt for the perfect LPVS.

Looking for Readily Available Assets

One of the easiest ways to identify a potentially attractive LPVS is to check the amount of cash and marketable securities a company has on hand. Many good LPVSs have a very high percentage of cash relative to their stock price; often, the cash exceeds the current market value of the stock. Yes, it's true; there are times when the cash value of a company can significantly exceed the market price of its shares. One would think this might be an absolute reason to buy these shares, and very often it is, but there are circumstances in which an extremely large cash holding may not truly indicate that the stock is, in reality, cheap.

Take Note

One of the easiest ways to identify a potentially attractive LPVS is to check the amount of cash and marketable securities a company has on hand.

Some companies may have significant obligations, which commit that cash to projects that may, in fact, not be good business prospects. There may be large commitments that have been made by the company, and the cash, while still in the company's possession, may be committed to projects that may not have great upside potential. For example, many cash-rich biotech companies appear to be financially well off, but in reality are burning cash at extremely high rates, meaning that the cash will probably be spent before any tangible revenues or sales are generated by the company. The large cash possession may in fact be far too small for the company to accomplish its desired goals and are of no real value to a shareholder unless their project becomes a success.

If, in fact, a company is forced to go out into the marketplace to get more cash to continue its work on its various research projects, it may be forced to give out sizable equity positions in order to attract new additional capital. The company will usually have shown a very long history of red ink, and any attempt to raise fresh equity dollars very likely will come at a high price, thereby significantly reducing the underlying value of the company on a per-share basis. One of the greatest dangers a small company faces is a bloated capitalization, which often causes such a large overhang in the stock that any upside potential often becomes very difficult.

Take Note

One of the greatest dangers a small company faces is a bloated capitalization, which often causes such a large overhang in the stock that any upside potential often becomes very difficult.

There are many other commitments a company might have in the ordinary course of its business that could significantly draw down the company's cash reserves—commitments the company might have to joint ventures, pension plans, employee stock ownership plans, and so on. One very simple reason a large cash position may not stay intact is that management may decide to "feast at the trough" and draw down the cash position through salaries and expenses that may or may not be justified. It seems that cash has a real attraction to greedy, unscrupulous management who will try to make a public company's cash their own.

Digging Deeper

Even with this in the back of your mind, you can still find many small companies that have significant cash hoards that could be of great value to a shareholder. How does one find these companies that have very large cash hoards and a stock price significantly below the underlying cash per share? According to Joel Marcus (a long-term low-priced stock specialist and market maker in hundreds of low-priced issues), "...the easiest way to spot the stocks that are obviously out of whack is to watch CNBC in the morning and see some of the significant premarket declines in companies that have just experienced some negative news." He further states, "...the desire of mainstream Wall Street to flush out their stock positions which have experienced a major disappointment is overwhelming." Many holders of the shares will just sell virtually regardless of price. These stocks basically become "corpses." But even a corpse may have some value. Usually, the impetus of the selling will overwhelm even the company's value as a corpse, thereby creating an opportunity for the astute investor, who can identify the intrinsic value that may still be present.

Many times, a company may voluntarily cease the continuation of their R&D project due to failure or disappointments in a trial or another company's announcement that it has developed a product that is superior to the product that they are trying to develop. An astute management team may also realize that, despite the cash reserves, the company may have to take the proposed product through testing and trials, which is very expensive and could take years to accomplish. As Joel Marcus stated, "A company like Amgen or Genentech could throw many millions of dollars at a project without hesitation, making it all that much more difficult for a small company to compete." Of course, there are exceptions, and some small biotech companies do succeed and prosper, but an astute management, when they realize they are hitting a wall, may choose

to terminate the current operation and look for greener pastures
for their cash.

The Importance of Knowing Management

After discovering a beaten-down situation with a lot of cash remaining, it is wise to interview management to try to understand their
thinking going forward to make an educated determination as to
their future direction for the company. As a general rule, Mr. Marcus
states, "You must determine the percentage of stock ownership of
the management and insiders in determining whether there will be
a real effort to improve the condition of the company going forward and the stock price. If the insiders and management do not
own a significant piece of the company's stock, they may be more
interested in making the company's cash their own rather than
hoping to make their money through a reappreciation through the
company's beaten-down shares."

Concluding Thoughts

EXEG is a classic example of a stock that was trading at about half its
cash value after it had decided to exit its original business activity. By
developing a new game plan and a new alignment in management
over the years, Opko Health (its current name) is now listed on the
American Stock Exchange and trades around the $4 level.

What You See Isn't Always What You Get: WQN Inc. (WQNI)

No matter how good a potential LPVS may appear to be, there are
always circumstances and events that could prevent it from becoming a winner. No matter how much research and analysis one puts
into a situation, unexpected events and circumstances may ruin the
situation. Because of the unknown and uncertainties of investing in
LPVSs, investors must make sure they adequately diversify their holdings of these types of securities, knowing that a portion of these companies may ultimately fail for reasons beyond their control. Over the
years, I've had several situations that I believed to be almost a sure
thing; yet, for one reason or another, they did not work out the way
I had hoped.

Take Note

Because of the unknown and uncertainties of investing in LPVSs, investors must make sure they adequately diversify their holdings of these types of securities, knowing that a portion of these companies may ultimately fail for reasons beyond their control.

In order to prevent one of these unexpected negative situations from having a major detrimental effect on your portfolio, you must stay balanced with the amount of money you invest in any one particular situation. The reality is that a big winner on an LPVS can often produce profits many times the initial investment, whereas a bad LPVS situation will never trade below zero. Therefore, if a situation does go bad, and the number of shares owned was in the proper ratio (relative size), it shouldn't affect the overall performance of your portfolio, considering the fact that the winners you will most likely have should offset the occasional losses you will surely experience. Remember, a diversified portfolio of LPVSs is essential.

Take Note

A diversified portfolio of low-priced value stocks is essential.

A Lesson Learned

One such situation, which I thought for a variety of reasons qualified as a very attractive LPVS, was a company called Worldquest Communications (symbol: WQNI). Worldquest (see Figure 11.2) started trading publicly in early 2000 and traded as high as $36 a share. Being in the "voice over Internet protocol (IP)" and international calling card business, it was a benefactor of the Internet boom of the late 1990s until early 2000. Shortly after the bloom came off the rose and the Internet bubble burst, the stock immediately began to decline precipitously, and by the end of 2000 was trading in the $2 range. It continued to trade in this range for almost the next five years, with occasional spikes to as high as $7 and as low as $1.25. During

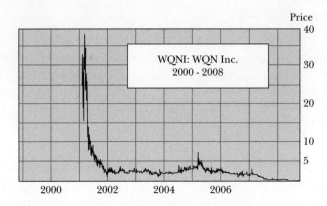

Figure 11.2 WQNI: WQN Inc., 2000–2008

Data source: Yahoo! Finance, Nasdaq.com

this period, the company was selling at well under its cash value and seemed to be making progress in the hot "voice over IP" space.

The Fall

Well-known investment gurus such as Peter Lynch acquired sizable positions in WQNI shares. During this time, the company had a relatively small capitalization with virtually no debt and fewer than 6 million shares outstanding, much of it held by management. The management of WQNI was and still is fairly aggressive and engaged in merger and acquisition activities on a regular basis. Once again, the company was in a relatively glamorous field of voice over IP and that in conjunction with an aggressive style by management made the company's shares look cheap and somewhat glamorous, with a possible major upside potential. In 2000, the company was selling at about $2 share, with a large cash position and a significant holding in another glamorous small company called VOIP, Inc. (VOIP). The underlying shares that WQNI owned in VOIP represented more value than the total WQNI stock capitalization and WQNI itself held in excess of $2 a share in cash. With all this going for it, I believed that WQNI certainly appeared to be a good LPVS candidate, considering that its shares were selling at less than half its intrinsic value at the time. But, as bad luck would have it, the management systematically made improper moves and got themselves involved in deals that blew up in their face at the time, including real estate investments. They got involved with unsavory promoters and quickly dissipated much of their cash, while their large investment in VOIP precipitously fell into the toilet (pricewise). While I believe there may still be hope for this situation and it might turn around, right now it is certainly an example of a good LPVS, on paper, gone bad.

Concluding Thoughts

Remember, even companies that appear to be dirt cheap and have unusually good upside/potential can ultimately become worthless due to circumstances beyond the control of management or economic circumstance. Nothing is a sure thing (one can never know for sure). Losers will certainly be a part of your LPVS reality, especially if you are properly diversified, meaning you are holding several different LPVS selections. Don't let these setbacks shake you. They are part of the game, and to be expected.

> **Take Note**
>
> Even companies that appear to be dirt cheap and have unusually good upside/potential can ultimately become worthless.

Visible but Volatile: Airline Stocks

While most LPVSs that turn out to be major winners are companies you have probably never heard of and do not command the notoriety and following of the media, you will often find LPVS candidates that were major companies that have suffered business setbacks, which very likely can and will be resolved. Most people would be surprised to learn that well-known companies—household names—have on occasion fallen into the LPVS category and given the bold investor returns that would be considered nothing short of staggering. Take, for example, American Airlines Corp. (AMR), the world's largest airline. It was recently one of the best LPVS plays ever (see Figure 11.3).

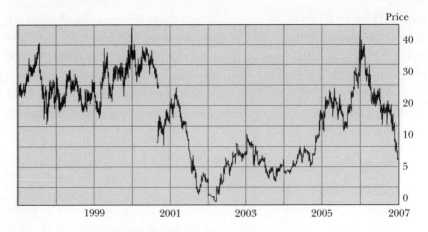

Figure 11.3 AMR: AMR Corporation, 1998–2008

Data source: Yahoo! Finance, Nasdaq.com

AMR

When most of the airline stocks were getting into serious financial trouble due to high fuel costs, a reluctant traveling public due to 9/11, labor unrest, and changing bankruptcy laws, American Airlines stock got pummeled along with the rest of the publicly traded airline stocks. In March 2003, AMR stock traded down as low as $1.25 a share on millions of shares of volume. Yes, there was risk involved, and yes, several of the airline companies did wind up going bankrupt, but most of those did not have the underlying fundamental value AMR possessed.

When the dust finally settled in one year, the stock appreciated over 1,000 percentage points, to more than $17 a share by January 2004. By March 2006, the stock traded in excess of $29 a share. Then, less than another year later, in January 2007, the stock traded up to a high of $41 a share, for a 3,200 percent potential return.

Easily Accessible Stocks

Now, remember, we are talking about American Airlines, not some obscure stock that was unknown or off everyone's radar. I'm not saying that you would have been smart enough to buy the absolute low, or sell the high, but with enormous profit potential like this, it just might have been enough to justify placing a small percentage of your more speculative assets into these types of investments. Even if you bought an equal amount of a few of the beaten-down airline stocks, including Delta, United, U.S. Airways, Continental, and others, the return on just a few would have been worth it. I bought Delta in bankruptcy for approximately $0.55 and traded it out for a couple hundred percent points profit. I made a nice LPVS return on even a company that ultimately went into bankruptcy.

Concluding Thoughts

Situations with well-known companies that ultimately turn around can return gains of several thousand percentage points. This is why the risk-reward in LPVSs is so pronounced. One would be hard pressed to name a conventional Wall Street recommendation in which the profit potential is so significant. If you're going to take risk of equity investment, make sure the rewards are potentially far greater than the risk. Even if several of these situations didn't work out and, in fact, traded down to zero, by my staying balanced, diversified, and disciplined, the extremely rewarding potential results easily offset the wipe-outs.

Take Note

By my staying balanced, diversified, and disciplined, the extremely rewarding potential results easily offset the wipe-outs.

12

Starting Your Treasure Hunt

Y ou've read this book, analyzed my theories and beliefs, read the examples of my experiences in the world of low-priced value stocks (LPVSs), and you are now convinced that it makes sense to proceed into this arena of investment. You want to begin, but you have a feeling of uneasiness—a feeling that you may not be up to the task of going it alone. There are many uncertainties, potential pitfalls, and risks, all of which you may feel unprepared to handle. The fact of the matter is that you may well be correct in your fears and concerns. I sometimes take for granted my ability to see and analyze many things that many other individuals may not recognize or truly understand. This is not to say that I am far smarter than others, but when it comes to understanding the realities and intricacies of maneuvering around Wall Street, it is probably fair to say that my training and experience, by far, exceeds that of the average investor. What to me seems apparent and obvious, to others may not appear that way at all.

Look around You

As I have explained, good ideas for LPVS candidates are literally all around us. That great piece of software you just bought, that new fast-food franchise you enjoyed so much, the wonderful experience you had with that online retailer from whom you just bought something, and so on, are all potential companies that you might want to invest in. Warren Buffett became a billionaire investor buying into companies he liked. He liked them because he felt he could understand what they did and how they did it. Companies such as Coca-Cola, Johnson & Johnson, Budweiser, American Express, and Procter & Gamble are some of his enormous holdings—all companies he felt he readily understood. Fortunately for him, he can afford to invest millions and even billions into these selections and hopefully make an above-market return when he is correct. When you are managing, literally, many billions of dollars, your investment objectives are far different than those of an LPVS investor. Warren could never and would never get involved in companies that had minuscule market capitalizations. There would be little or no point to it since the numeric dollar returns would be essentially meaningless to his multibillion-dollar portfolio. Due to this reality, most successful money managers don't involve themselves in LPVS investing exclusively. And frankly, there aren't enough quality LPVS situations to utilize the large amount of dollars available for this type of investing, relative to the size of the funds they have under management.

Take Note

Warren Buffet became a billionaire investor buying into companies he liked.

Getting Out There

The lack of professional money managers playing in the LPVS arena makes it a very inviting opportunity for the individual. Going it alone as a novice investor, however, can be nerve-racking and treacherous, but certainly not impossible. I earnestly encourage all who have the discipline, confidence, and financial wherewithal to cautiously approach the world of LPVS investing and give it a try. I believe the potential rewards, by far, outweigh the risks of making serious mistakes. For those of you who are not as confident in your own ability, there may be a few alternatives available to you that could allow for some of your capital to be invested in LPVS situations by others. Your effort in this area could be to simply find a qualified adviser to take you by the hand to begin your journey.

Most money managers invest in companies with relatively high market capitalizations, but there are a few managers who do work in the lower-end market-capitalization environment. While I know of several small- and mid-cap money managers, few quality money managers specialize in LPVS (nano)-type securities exclusively. Beware of slick penny-stock brokers who claim to be low-priced stock experts. Many stockbrokers who work in the low-priced arena are in fact affiliated with the proverbial "bucket shops" or "boiler rooms," whose primary objective is to make your dollars their own, so your best bet would be to find a small-cap/micro-cap specialist with a proven track record of investing successfully in lower-priced quality issues. Check out the portfolios of these micro-cap money managers and mutual funds and see if they venture into the very small-capitalization stocks often traded on the bulletin board or pink sheets. If they do, see how well they have performed and/or contact their sales organizations and ask them if they have a more targeted LPVS special situation fund or something close to it. If they don't, see if they can recommend a money manager who might specialize in these types of investments, but do your homework because finding a qualified LPVS money manager may, in fact, be more difficult than finding a few good LPVS situations to invest in yourself. The decision is ultimately yours.

Take Note

Finding a qualified LPVS money manager may, in fact, be more difficult than finding a few good LPVS situations to invest in yourself.

Stay Positive

Don't get discouraged. Ask around and you can probably find some astute qualified LPVS trader who is having some success in his LPVS investing efforts and could certainly use some additional working capital to expand his efforts. People like this are out there, and good deals can readily be established in a professional businesslike fashion. Make sure you do your due diligence, though, if you go into partnership with any person, and establish your arrangement in writing, with proper counsel. Remember, Wall Street is a highly regulated environment and you must be sure not to make any arrangements that do not fully comply with federal, state, and local laws. Get references and track records of the people you intend to work with or financially back. Establish all the terms of your arrangement, including profit and loss sharing, entry and exit strategies for your investment with the manager, conflicts of interest, concentration of positions, and so on. Try to find an LPVS adviser who comes recommended by someone you know and trust. Remember, the risks of this type of relationship may in fact be more formidable than the investing and trading risks themselves, so proceed intelligently.

Over the years, I have been asked repeatedly to set up LPVS investments for my friends and associates. While this possibility has always seemed plausible, it would put me potentially in a very conflicted position with my own personal trading and investing. So, unless the amount of outside funding were significant enough, it would hardly pay to restrict my own LPVS activities for the benefit of other people, which may seem selfish, but this reality is why so few successful LPVS money managers and traders look for outside capital. If I were to raise the multimillions necessary to make the endeavor economically worthwhile, without too much hassle, the sheer size of the fund might make it too difficult to be as efficient as a smaller, more closely managed entity. While I have not totally ruled out the possibility of setting up a public LPVS fund, the verdict is still out.

In any event, I firmly believe it is worth the effort to be involved in this aspect of the equities market. Whether you are going ahead yourself or with the assistance of a trusted confidant, you are engaging in an enterprise that should throw off significant rewards, especially if you follow the disciplines, stay diversified, do your homework, and stay within your risk and financial parameters. Incidentally, LPVS investments make great cocktail party topics of discussion. Everyone loves to hear about a great undiscovered investment that rose extraordinarily in price—it's what dreams are made of.

Take Note

Follow the disciplines, stay diversified, do your homework, and stay within your risk and financial parameters.

Start Your Treasure Hunt

Making money in today's market is more difficult than perhaps at any other time in Wall Street's history. Today's market participants are far more sophisticated and aggressive than at any other time in the past. High-tech computerization, electronic access, and transparency coupled with some of the smartest and most brilliant people have made competing in the Wall Street arena very difficult at best. Trying to out-trade, out-think, or out-muscle the powers that be is a futile effort. Add to this the fact that you can't expect real help from the financial community because their main objective is to make your money theirs, and things get complicated. If you don't take control of your investments, you'll be the last to know what is really going on with your money. Don't subject yourself to the sheer nonsense of the mainstream media and orchestrated baloney of the so-called Wall Street experts. There may just be a better way to earn above-average or even spectacular returns within the investment world.

As I have attempted to demonstrate, the best way I think there is to "beat the (Wall Street) system" is to avoid it as much as possible. Invest in securities that are not closely followed by the mainstream Wall Street community and therefore not as controlled by them. The forgotten, overlooked, ignored, and out-of-favor stocks that your broker will virtually never bring to your attention just may be the gems you were looking for. Fabulous opportunities exist in the underbelly of the financial markets and are awaiting the motivated treasure hunter to identify them, the attractive candidates, and begin reaping the rewards. Simply stated, "go where they're not"—accumulate the booty (stock) and wait for the world to discover what you have already found. Then, be gracious, and allow them to buy your booty at significantly higher prices. If you are able to follow this logic, life can be very good, indeed!

Index